THE COURAGE TO WALK AWAY

MOVE ON AFTER **INFIDELITY** BY
MOURNING WHAT YOU **LOST,**
IDENTIFYING YOUR **RELATIONSHIP NEEDS,**
AND **EMPOWERING** YOURSELF
FOR **THE FUTURE**

LISA BRATEMAN, LCSW
WITH KAREN MOLINE

ULYSSES PRESS

To Jordan, Brett, and Eva

* * *

Published by:
Ulysses Press
PO Box 3440
Berkeley, CA 94703
www.ulyssespress.com

ISBN: 978-1-64604-558-7
Library of Congress Control Number: 2023943926

Printed in the United States
10 9 8 7 6 5 4 3 2 1

Acquisitions editor: Kierra Sondereker
Managing editor: Claire Chun
Editor: Phyllis Elving
Proofreader: Sherian Brown
Front cover design: Amy King
Artwork: © marukopum/shutterstock.com
Layout: Winnie Liu

CONTENTS

INTRODUCTION 5

PART I: What Really Happened? 11

CHAPTER 1: The Initial Shock of Betrayal 12

What Is Infidelity? 12

Why Are People Unfaithful? 12

The Three Kinds of Infidelity 13

Finding Out Your Partner Was Unfaithful 18

CHAPTER 2: Raging Emotions in the Aftermath............................ 25

Identifying Shock.. 25

Identifying Anger 27

Identifying Trust 33

Identifying Depression 38

Identifying Anxiety 41

Identifying Grief and Sadness 45

Identifying Strength and Courage 48

CHAPTER 3: New Circumstances and a Changed Lifestyle........... 50

Identify Your Losses and Lifestyle Changes 51

The Fear of Loneliness... 58

What You *Won't* Miss in the Future 62

PART II: Healing from Infidelity—Strategies That Work..................... 65

CHAPTER 4: Sexual Infidelity 66

Your Sex Life before Sexual Infidelity 67

Your Response to Sexual Infidelity.. 69

CHAPTER 5: Emotional Infidelity 80

The Roots of Emotional Infidelity 80

CHAPTER 6: Financial Infidelity 90

The Red Flags of Financial Infidelity 91

Financial Repercussions 92

Emotional Repercussions 99

CHAPTER 7: Healing from the Fallout with Friends, Family, and Children 104

Dealing with Your Friends 104

Dealing with Your Family 116

Dealing with Children 122

CHAPTER 8: Strategies for Stress Relief 127

What Stress Can Do to Your Body 128

The Stress Relief You Need 129

Creating a Stress-Busting Plan 138

PART III: Empowerment 140

CHAPTER 9: Turning Loss Into Opportunity 141

Shifting from the Past to Peace of Mind 143

Your Future Relationships 154

Moving Forward with Hope 161

IN CONCLUSION 165

ACKNOWLEDGMENTS 166

ABOUT THE AUTHOR 167

INTRODUCTION

"Things don't have to last forever to matter."

—Mare of Easttown

There is life after betrayal.

"I came home from a business trip and realized he was gone," said Alexandra, one of my clients. "Not gone as in he's at the supermarket, or our favorite coffee shop, but gone as in…he packed up and left. I first noticed the espresso maker was missing, then the ottoman that matched the chair sitting sadly alone in the living room. I ran into the bedroom and saw a note on my computer screen. The note had fifteen words that said, 'I'm with Olivia now. I didn't mean for it to happen, but it did. Sorry.' After ten years together, I got fifteen words!"

Even for someone as wronged as Alexandra, there *is* life after the heart-sinking moment of shock she had when she read those fifteen words—followed by confusion, rage, questions, sadness, anxiety, humiliation, and the end to the life dreams she and her ex had once shared with so much love.

If you are dealing with the aftermath of a painful and life-altering breakup—made worse by the emotional turmoil when trust has been breached and vows have been broken— you are not alone. You may already know that nearly 50 percent of all marriages in the US end in separation or divorce. Not all are caused by infidelity, of course, but that's up there as one of the primary causes (or perhaps as the nail in the coffin of unhappiness). The figures are sobering. An estimated 41 percent of first marriages, 60 percent of second marriages, and 73 percent of third marriages in the US end in divorce.[1] In fact, there is a divorce in this country every forty-two *seconds*—the time it likely took you to read this paragraph! And these statistics don't include all the couples living together without being married.

Yet there is no reason for you to suffer when you can take steps toward a healing that you might not yet think to be possible.

---

[1] Divorce Statistics: Over 115 Studies, Facts and Rates for 2022," Wilkinson & Finkbeiner, https://www.wf -lawyers.com/divorce-statistics-and-facts.

I've been a therapist for more than twenty-three years, and I've counseled hundreds of individuals and couples during and after breakups. During our sessions together, my clients often ask the same questions about their own behavior and that of their exes. The one thing I've said to each of them is that at some point the dust will settle and they'll be able to look back at their relationship objectively to identify issues and patterns, enabling them to move forward to all the possibilities a new and empowered future will bring.

I also tell them how important it is to have some kind of help on their journey toward healing. That is why I've created this workbook. Time and again I've heard a variation of the following story from clients:

> "I grew up in the suburbs, and when I got married twenty years ago there was no place for me to talk to anyone except with my friends—and they were often as confused by life as I was. I would have really been helped by expert, concrete suggestions when I knew divorce was the only solution to my marriage, which had become stifling and unhappy.

> "Even more important, it would have been a huge help, after I found out my partner had cheated and my heart was broken and I was a wreck, to have been given an opening to a place where I could heal without feeling like I was burdening my friends and loved ones with my troubles. To have found a companion that would not only have reassured me about everything that had happened but would also have given me strategies and tools to help me get over my breakup."

Consider this workbook to be the companion you can turn to after betrayal. Whether what happened to you was sexual infidelity (your partner was physically intimate with another person), emotional infidelity (your partner became emotionally connected and dependent upon another person, often without physical intimacy), financial infidelity (you discover that your partner has been secretly dealing with money issues), or a combination of these three, this book will help you heal in a similar manner to therapy sessions by letting you express how you feel in a safe way. In private. Whenever you need to. For your eyes only.

You'll be given the space you need to express your emotions. You might be holding it together during the day so you can be productive at work or calm and steady in front of the children or with other family members, but within these pages you can have all the cathartic meltdowns you need. It's okay to be furious. It's okay to vent. It's also okay to have a pity party because what happened to you was truly painful!

Much as psychologist Elizabeth Kubler-Ross described five different reactions for dealing with dying, there are reactions you can expect when dealing with the upheaval caused by infidelity and the end of a relationship:

SHOCK. When you're blindsided and in chaos, with emotions riding high and flying all over the place, shock is to be expected. When you finally land, everything that's happening can hit you very hard.

DENIAL. You can't believe this is happening to you.

ANGER. Once the dust settles, rage arrives. Who wouldn't be enraged that trust has been violated in such a humiliating way?

DIVISION OF PROPERTY. This can create another sense of loss as you divvy up who gets what. Your financial circumstances might now be different, and you might be suffering from having to move out of the home you loved to a smaller place, away from your friends, with a longer commute and no nearby grocery stores. And even if your financial circumstances aren't changed, your emotional circumstances certainly are.

DEPRESSION AND ANXIETY. Most people feel some level of situational depression when their marriage ends, and they are sad and grieving about what has happened. You might expect to have some level of anxiety about your own situation.

ACCEPTANCE. As time goes on, you can see much more clearly—you're coping, you're striving, you're acknowledging the positives about your new situation, and you're also able to look with a clearer sense of what happened, which can inform your future.

SELF-KNOWLEDGE. Part of the healing process is looking back at who you were then and being better able to know who you are now—to see how you've changed and how empowered you've become.

HOPE. In this final stage, you have processed your losses and are ready to move on. Now it's about creating the life you want—on your terms.

***

You'll notice that these reactions aren't numbered. That's because they are different for everyone and are nonlinear, meaning that they don't necessarily follow a certain order. (If they did, healing would be a bit easier to predict!) While the first reaction to infidelity is usually shock, for some there is very little denial—instead, there's a sad but welcome relief that their suspicions have been confirmed.

Others get angry and depressed, then feel better and accept what happened, begin to get their lives in order, and make plans for the future—until they are triggered by something and go right back to anger and depression. Finding out details you wish you hadn't known, weeks and months later—that perhaps the infidelity was not just with one person but many, or that there were secret bank accounts—makes your feelings change in response.

I've had clients who've been stuck in unhappiness for fifteen years, defining themselves solely as the wronged partner, and they've needed intervention from professional counseling before they could feel better. But I've also counseled people such as Adam, who said, "I have to admit we both wanted out, and now that it's happened, I realize I kind of went through my divorce emotionally while we were still married! We had both checked out before she cheated. And the day she moved out was such a relief that the first thing I did was put all my clothes where hers had been in the closet. That was my way of taking a deep breath and telling myself that this is the first day of the rest of my life."

I want to reassure you that there's no right or wrong way for you to feel.

HOW THIS WORKBOOK WILL HELP YOU

This book is a starting point for your new life. As you move through these pages over time, you'll create progressive responses enabling you to identify your own unique emotional patterns and issues you weren't aware of before, enabling you to not only manage them now but to recognize them in the future. Each chapter builds upon the previous one, offering exercises and strategies to take you through the processes of mourning for what you've lost, examining your behavior and needs, and clarifying what you want in the future.

I do want you to realize that when talking or thinking about difficult topics, people almost always avoid what's hard. If there are specific questions that might unwittingly push your buttons or shut you down, make you flustered or even angry, then pass them by for now—but be sure to come back to them at some point. The questions that upset you the most might provide the answers that will actually *help* you the most—because they're about issues you have avoided confronting.

During therapy sessions, I'll often ask a tough question and then tell my clients not to answer it that day but to put it in their back pocket, and we'll see what happens during our next session. This can begin the process of understanding. What is it about the question that feels hard? Sometimes they don't even have to answer to know what's at the heart of the problem. This sets the stage for them to start dealing with issues that may have been untouchable or that they weren't yet ready to confront.

After all, the only one who can push past your defense mechanisms is *you*. And this workbook is here to help you do that. You'll be able to do these things:

- Stop judging yourself or beating yourself up for past mistakes.
- Put a stop to the painful triggers that take you back to the past.
- Accept that it takes two people to make a relationship work—or not work—even if you were the wronged party and the victim of betrayal.
- Rebuild your confidence. This is especially important, as one of the questions I'm always asked is "When will I feel better?" I wish I could say that there is one irrefutable answer to this question, but there isn't. Every person and every situation is different, so there's no specific timeline for getting over infidelity—and *your* timeline is the only one that matters.
- What I *can* say is that one day you will wake up and no longer have that dread in the pit of your stomach. Perhaps there will be an aha moment when you think, "I'm looking forward to what lies ahead instead of just trying to get through the day." Or the changes in how you feel have been so small and incremental that you don't realize they've happened—until suddenly you do!
- Most of all, what I hope you get out of this workbook is the firm belief that there is life after infidelity—and that you can be hopeful about it. I'm going to show you that you don't need to take the good memories away, even though it can be difficult to remember how much you and your ex were once in love.

I know how hard it can be to envision happiness again, especially when your breakup first happens. But many times there is a much better life waiting for you, with or without a new partner. A life that you will be living on *your* terms, charging toward new possibilities and opportunities instead of living in the betrayal every day.

Nothing can change what has happened to you in the past. When pain is unendurable, you think it will never go away, but eventually it lessens. Ask any woman who gave birth without an epidural. The pain was horrific, but as soon as the baby was born, that pain became just a memory. If it didn't, no one would ever have a second child!

You are going to be able to say much more than, "I survived infidelity." You're going to be able to say, "I now know how to enhance my life. I am stronger, smarter, more self-assured, and more open to whatever gets thrown my way."

You're also going to shift your thinking and rid yourself of any sense of failure. Your relationship might have ended in a way you never expected, but *you* didn't fail. This is what happened with Alexandra. When her anger subsided, she was able to look back on her marriage, not as it was when her husband's infidelity ended it, but from her new status as a woman who has transitioned into who she wants to be, doing what she wants to do now.

"You know what?" she said to me. "We were married for ten years, and nine of them were really good, and the last one totally sucked. But the truth is that not every relationship is meant to be forever. Of course, I hoped that my marriage would have lasted till death do us part, but even though it ended, this doesn't mean it was a mistake. I have amazing children and amazing friends who love me, and right now I've learned some pretty fantastic lessons about myself and how to love myself even more. Finally I know what I truly want and deserve."

Change will come, and you will feel better. You will no longer define yourself by the infidelity.

Now that you're ready to take action, *let's get going*.

PART I

WHAT REALLY HAPPENED?

CHAPTER 1

THE INITIAL SHOCK OF BETRAYAL

"If you marry a man who cheats on his wife, you'll be married to a man who cheats on his wife."

— Ann Landers

WHAT IS INFIDELITY?

According to the *Merriam-Webster* dictionary, infidelity is "the act or fact of having a romantic or sexual relationship with someone other than one's husband, wife, or partner."

Even if your relationship has been rocky for some time, finding out that your partner has betrayed you is devastating. Infidelity is a betrayal. Most secrets your partner kept from you are damaging, although some—such as getting a mistress pregnant—are worse than others. But it's always better to know the truth than not to know—because then you can deal with your current reality. (If, on the other hand, you decide to stay together after infidelity, for whatever reason—not breaking up the family, not wanting to be alone— this is not the book for you!) And in many cases, infidelity is only one of the reasons for a once-loving relationship to end.

WHY ARE PEOPLE UNFAITHFUL?

This is a question my clients ask all the time. There are as many reasons why people are unfaithful as there are fish in the sea. Or rather, the reasons aren't really reasons; they're *rationalizations*.

Ask a man about being unfaithful, and then ask a woman. Sometimes you'll get very different answers. In my experience, I've found that men are seeking answers to the questions "Do I still have it?" and "Can I still attract a younger woman as I get older?"

In other words, cheating for men is sometimes about needing an ego stroke or a boost to their morale. Other reasons I've heard from men are that they seek sexual variety, their partnership isn't satisfying, or their wives are no longer interested in sex.

For women, I've found that it's more about missing the emotional connection with their partner. Sex is a part of it, to be sure, but just as important or even more so is how close they felt to their partner, and how they assumed their partner had their back—but then found out otherwise.

I often wonder if so many people are unfaithful nowadays because it's literally so much easier to do so than it was before social media and burner phones. A person might be mindlessly flirting with someone via text, but when they get an encouraging response, they reply. And the moment they press send, there's no way to undo the potential damage.

Sometimes, though, people are unfaithful because they actually want to get caught. They don't know how to say "I want out" or "We really have a problem here." This isn't a passive-aggressive move. Rather, it is one of the most destructive ways to get the attention of a partner and make them face the issues they've been avoiding.

THE THREE KINDS OF INFIDELITY

The three different kind of infidelity I see in my private practice are sexual, emotional, and financial. Sometimes two or even all three kinds of infidelity play a part in ending a relationship.

SEXUAL INFIDELITY

The most clear-cut kind of infidelity is when your partner is physically intimate with someone else.

Couples need to state their expectations about sexual infidelity early on in their relationship. I've counseled people who were distraught after finding out that the person they were dating was still seeing and sleeping with others, but they admitted they hadn't yet had the "Are we exclusive?" conversation. While it might be uncomfortable to realize this, a person can't truly be considered unfaithful if the couple hasn't yet agreed to be monogamous. When couples assume they are monogamous without having had that conversation, one person is often going to be disappointed and heartbroken.

Business trips are often the perfect cover for betrayal. While waiting for her husband at the bar of a fancy hotel in Chicago, Angelica sat down near an older man wearing an expensive suit and a thick gold wedding ring and ordered a Diet Coke. "Are you working?" the man asked her. She looked very confused, and the man excused himself and hurried away. "What was that about?" she asked the bartender. The bartender explained that "working girls" usually ordered only a Diet Coke or a club soda so they didn't have to pay for an alcoholic drink, as one of their soon-to-be customers would put it on their tab instead. "Wow, am I naïve!" Angelica said, and they laughed. But she didn't really find it funny at all.

Did your partner commit sexual infidelity? Yes ☐ No ☐

What were the circumstances?

_____

_____

_____

_____

EMOTIONAL INFIDELITY

It's not uncommon to be attracted to other people. We've all lusted after movie stars or had fantasies about that super-buff trainer in the gym. Who didn't have a crush on someone as a teen, or in the decades beyond? Being attracted to someone is a fact of life and can bring fun and joy into your heart, whether it's you crushing on someone, or someone crushing on you or your partner.

In other words, when you meet or see someone who you find attractive, it's totally okay to run with some fantasies in your own head. Those are your private thoughts. You're not acting on them. You're giving yourself permission to be human—and this is *not* emotional infidelity. It's what you do with that attraction that counts.

Emotional infidelity happens when your partner become emotionally attached to and confides in someone *other than you.* Or when they act upon a fantasy in deeds short of having a sexual relationship. Often emotional infidelity isn't planned, especially for those who don't want to have an affair but are feeling vulnerable and are looking for something that's lacking in their current relationship. Because there's no sex involved, they think it isn't really a betrayal. But it is!

This often happens in the workplace, where colleagues need to talk to each other about their daily business. Over time, what had been a benign and professional relationship can deepen into shared confidences and even sexting. (This is where the tired cliché of "My wife/husband doesn't understand me" can pop up.) Sending a colleague texts about work issues or wishing their kids luck in a soccer tournament is to be expected. Sending them flirtatious text messages is not.

Proving emotional infidelity is different and subtler than proving sexual infidelity. Sometimes it can be hard to understand the difference between a friendship with someone—a work colleague, for example, who's very chatty and perhaps shares a bit too much about themself but isn't invested in anything profound with your ex—and a deep, ongoing, in-person or text/phone relationship that involves sharing intimate details. Or there can be a kind of dreamy look or change in your partner's voice when talking about that person. A case of sexual infidelity initially based on lust can become emotional infidelity as well if a strong attachment evolves.

CASE STUDY: HOW EMOTIONAL INFIDELITY CAN START

Here's one example. Andreas had been married to Sonya for twelve years, and all he wanted from his wife was to be heard. He felt she'd stopped listening to him, because she had an all-too-common habit of checking her texts when he was trying to have an important conversation with her. When a new employee named Brittney wanted to hear what he did last weekend or that his mother had to be put in assisted living or what his goals and aspirations were, he eagerly confided in her. Eventually Brittney emotionally replaced Sonya; she became Andreas's go-to person. She was the first person he'd call when he had a problem.

Sonya finally got wind of this situation when she glanced at Andreas's phone one day and saw photos of Brittney with her friends on vacation. They weren't sexual images, but they were personal images, not what you'd normally send to a colleague. The couple had a huge fight, with Sonya hurt and Andreas defensive.

***

Emotional infidelity can be as painful as sexual infidelity, or even more so. It's easier to understand a purely physical one-night stand than to know that your partner's innermost thoughts have been shared with someone else. That can be devastating.

Did your partner commit emotional infidelity?   *Yes* ☐ *No* ☐

In what way?

_____

_____

_____

_____

HOW COMMON IS INFIDELITY?

This is one statistic that will likely never be accurate, as most people don't admit to infidelity. But I can safely say that people betray their partners in one form or another more often than one would imagine.

The cliché is that men are unfaithful more often than women. But in my decades of experience as a couples therapist, I have found women to be just as unfaithful. With some couples, both are engaging in infidelity. And I've often seen that when both members of a married couple had been unfaithful with their first husband or wife, they end up being unfaithful with their next partners as well.

FINANCIAL INFIDELITY

Financial infidelity happens when your partner doesn't tell you the truth about their spending. It's all about hiding, dissembling, and keeping secrets.

This is the easiest kind of infidelity to prove. Suddenly a check bounces, a credit card is declined, you see charges for a hotel where your partner stayed on the weekend when he was supposed to be somewhere else entirely, or you get an email or a notice in the mail about an unpaid bill for a credit card you don't recognize. Maybe you discover that

THE **COURAGE** TO **WALK AWAY**

a password or a beneficiary has been changed, or you receive a bank alert when you are approaching your credit limit—though you haven't used that credit card in months. Perhaps your partner, who used to shop mostly at Walmart, is now buying online from upscale designers' stores. Or someone gets so angry at their partner that they go on a shopping spree and lie about how much everything cost. They might feel entitled to do so, but it's still financial infidelity!

If you were even a little suspicious, one misstep from the financial betrayer could open up a Pandora's box of expensive hits—both to your emotions and to your joint assets. Unlike sexual or emotional infidelity, this kind of infidelity can leave a devastating legacy of financial woes that will affect every aspect of how and where you live and deal with your expenses.

Couples need to be totally honest about their finances when their relationship gets serious. A person who moves in with someone who already owns a house will not share in the home equity, for example. And older people or those in second marriages will already have their own accounts and credit scores. A prenuptial or postnuptial agreement shouldn't be seen as a lack of trust, but rather as a smart way to protect your assets.

If you've clarified your money-management decisions and one of you still went off course and made decisions without including the other, that was financial infidelity. It's not so much about the money that was spent as it is a violation of what the two of you had agreed to. If there was an omission, it was in not admitting what had been spent or done. That's why even when your partner gave you an unexpected gift, if it put an unexpected dent in your finances, it was a form of financial infidelity. This kind of spending is a control issue. Even if you heard "But it's a good investment!" you had no way of knowing at that moment if that would turn out to be true.

Finding out that your partner had been spending money on a new girlfriend or boyfriend is a double whammy. Not only did your joint finances take a hit, especially if money is tight, but you were betrayed sexually as well.

Rita, a woman I once counseled, flipped this scenario on her soon-to-be ex, Adam. They had already separated, as he'd been having outside relationships for years and finally announced he was leaving to live with his mistress. Rita went on a vacation with their children, and Adam stayed in the family home while she was gone. He mistimed her return, however, and when she got back to the house, Adam's files were open on his computer. She was able to print out their joint financial records and, in a shocking find, all the offshore accounts he'd lied about to her attorney in order to lower his net worth and future child support payments. Let's just say that Adam wasn't happy when confronted with the truth—but adulterers rarely are!

Did your partner commit financial infidelity?   Yes ☐ No ☐

In what way?

_____

_____

_____

_____

FINDING OUT YOUR PARTNER WAS UNFAITHFUL

The loudest voice in the room is usually someone who knows they're wrong.

You will naturally become suspicious when your partner starts behaving differently. And once you're suspicious, in your mind everything becomes a lie.

Often people think they have proof of infidelity, but they won't say it to their partner at home. Then during a couples session they end up divulging everything they think they know! Their feeling is that the partner will be more truthful in a therapist's office—seeing it as neutral ground with me as a referee of sorts—than at home. A good therapist can keep people focused on one topic at a time, even one as painful as infidelity.

PHYSICAL SYMPTOMS OF A SHOCKING REVELATION

When the truth about a devastating, life-changing situation is revealed, you won't only have an emotional reaction but likely will have a physical reaction as well. I want to reassure you that any of the following symptoms are normal responses to a painful shock. However, if they persist over time—such as the feeling of panic morphing into ongoing panic attacks—please seek out medical advice.

- Intensified breathing, or finding it hard to breathe at all
- Crying or weeping
- Dizziness or fainting
- Hand-wringing
- Increased heart rate, with your chest feeling tight
- Hot or cold flashes or sweating
- Insomnia
- Losing track of time

- Weak muscles, buckling legs, trembling
- Nightmares
- Pacing
- Stomach clenching, or a persistent urge to use the bathroom
- Tingling in the tips of fingers or toes, or in the scalp
- Yelling
- Zoning out

List any of your own symptoms here:

_____   _____

_____   _____

_____   _____

COMMON WAYS PEOPLE DISCOVER INFIDELITY

CHANGES TO EVERYDAY BEHAVIOR. Such changes can be subtle, taking place over weeks or months. Or they can be drastic, as in the sudden announcement that your couch-potato partner wants to train for a marathon. Or your partner suddenly becomes more interested in grooming (new haircut, a liking for cologne) and the way they dress. They start going to the gym more often, and the workouts get longer. They're staying later at the office and working on weekends or holidays, traveling more for business, or are in an unusual number of "long meetings" where they can't be reached.

The following are examples that clients have shared in sessions on how they became suspicious about infidelity:

AVOIDED CONVERSATIONS. Your partner starts making excuses for not talking about certain things, when they know you want and need that talk to happen.

INTUITION. When you've lived with someone for some time, you get to know them pretty well. You can tell when they're ducking a situation due to shame (maybe they're embarrassed that they've gained weight), and when they're ducking the situation due to dishonesty (they're hiding something from you). You just feel it. Of course, intuition is notoriously inexact, but don't discount it entirely. Sometimes you might be right, and your partner is engaged in a full-blown affair, or sometimes it's just the beginning of one. Or sometimes your intuition is way off base.

CHANGES IN SEXUAL BEHAVIOR. You might be having a lot more sex (especially if your partner has a guilty conscience and wants you to believe everything is fine and they still find you desirable) or a lot less sex (because they're having more sex with someone else), paired with "I'm just too exhausted/busy/stressed right now for anything except sleep." Or they suddenly might want to experiment more in bed, and are insistent about it.

CREDIT CARDS. Anyone who had a bank account or credit cards prior to coupling up can keep the spending from these accounts hidden, although the breaches are obvious if notifications about passwords or credit limits come in the mail or online.

SOCIAL MEDIA. Today it's a whole new world of easy access and easy temptations. But it's also a whole new world of people forgetting that the internet is forever, and nothing is ever totally private. Many of those being disloyal thought they'd never get caught if they used Snapchat, where messages disappeared within twenty-four hours. But if they were screenshot, their messages became permanent.

TEXTING. It's so easy and so quick. It takes less time to send a text than to get a drink of water. Texting does away with impulse control, although experienced betrayers may think ahead and get a burner phone.

PHONE RECORDS. Even if information is deleted from one's phone, the carrier has a record of it if the phone is in your name.

DATING SITES. Those who have ideas about being unfaithful often create fake profiles and pretend they're single. Or they might have made a commitment to you but somehow forgot to delete their dating accounts and are still active on them. (This information can be difficult to find, however, if names are fake.)

TRACKING SOFTWARE. Such software can be installed without the recipient knowing, though this is not normally seen as ethical.

FRONT-DOOR OR IN-HOUSE CAMERAS. Cameras let you see who comes in and out. (It's pretty obvious that this has been installed, yet people still can forget it's there!)

ALEXA. This and other home devices can be used to record conversations.

WHAT SIGNS DID YOU SEE?

I've had clients who were suspicious by nature, accusing their partners of infidelity or other kinds of hurtful behavior that weren't true at all. Such relationships can become challenging—and not necessarily due to infidelity—unless the suspicious person gains a better understanding of how and why they feel suspicious. It often has to do with their own past relationships, or perhaps even watching what happened to their parents' marriage.

More often, though, when someone is suspicious they have good reason. It's what private investigators often say about their clients—that they already knew something is going on, and they hired a professional because they just wanted proof.

What I've heard countless times from couples in distress is the wife or husband saying to their partner, "JUST TELL ME! Not knowing is making me crazy! I've been seeing signs where there might not be signs, but you won't talk to me." Hopefully this will be the beginning of truth-telling, no matter how hurtful, so decisions can be made about how to deal with the consequences.

As painful as it might be to relive your own situation, writing it down in this workbook makes it a permanent record. Believe it or not, this can help you to see any patterns of unfortunate behavior in future relationships that you might have missed when you were first living through them.

Did you see any signs that made you suspicious?   *Yes* ☐ *No* ☐

If so, what were those signs? List them here.

_____

_____

_____

_____

What were the excuses you heard when you voiced your suspicions?

_____

_____

_____

_____

Were you accused of being paranoid or unkind, being told something such as "How could you say that?" or "Why don't you believe me?" or "I would never lie to you about something like that."

_____

What was the proof of the infidelity?

_____

_____

Describe the exact circumstances.

_____

_____

_____

_____

THE **COURAGE** TO **WALK AWAY**

What was your immediate reaction?

_____

_____

_____

Did you have a physical reaction? Yes ☐ No ☐

What were the physical symptoms?

_____

_____

_____

_____

_____

_____

How did they make you feel?

  Immediately after knowing:

_____

_____

  A few days later:

_____

_____

  A week or two later:

_____

_____

A month later:

_____

_____

Were you surprised by your reaction?   Yes ☐ No ☐

What was your partner's reaction?

_____

_____

_____

What was the worst reaction you experienced?

_____

_____

_____

Do you still flash back to that?   Yes ☐ No ☐

In the next chapter, you'll read about the feelings you might have after discovering and dealing with infidelity. And as you read and work through the rest of the exercises in this book, it's important to realize that you may never get the answers you desperately want to many of the questions and what-ifs you may be torturing yourself over. (These might be questions such as "Why did they do it?" or "What did the other person have that I didn't?") Part of healing is knowing that while the answers might not come, they just don't matter anymore—and that sometimes, in fact, getting the answers you crave can be more destructive than not getting them at all. Writing it all down in a private workbook such as this can be extremely healing.

CHAPTER 2

RAGING EMOTIONS IN THE AFTERMATH

"Cheating is easy. There's no swank to infidelity. To borrow against the trust someone has placed in you costs nothing at first. You get away with it, you take a little more and a little more until there is no more to draw on. Oddly, your hands should be full with all that taking but when you open them there's nothing there."

—Jeanette Winterson

This chapter describes the ways you might feel after betrayal and gives you the space to write down and express those feelings. In the next part of the book, you'll find suggestions and strategies for how to process these emotions.

As you're working through these sections and dealing with the tough stuff, keep on taking your emotional temperature. If it's too high, take a break! This workbook is for you to do at your own pace—it's not like a school assignment that you need to finish in one night. Take the time you need to identify and process your feelings.

IDENTIFYING SHOCK

All the clients I've counseled over the years have had the same initial reaction to proof of infidelity: shock. Even those who'd had their suspicions for quite some time, hoping they were wrong and wanting the situation to be resolved, were still shocked by the finality of the knowledge. And I have to say that many people initially don't want to believe the truth, and some will make excuses rather than accept what has been done. But it *was* done. There is no going back. There is just moving forward and facing the decisions that need to be made.

DESCRIBE HOW THE SHOCK MADE YOU FEEL

Circle the words that resonate the most with you.

- Alarmed
- Angry
- Appalled
- Astonished
- Beaten Down
- Bereft
- Betrayed
- Devastated
- Disbelieving

- Distressed
- Distraught
- Disturbed
- Enraged
- Flabbergasted
- Frightened
- Furious
- Insulted
- Jolted

- Numb
- Offended
- Outraged
- Relieved
- Staggered
- Stunned
- Surprised
- Taken Aback
- Upset

Because shock is usually unexpected and causes a surge in adrenaline, your body will have a physical reaction (as you read about in the previous chapter). You often hear "I wasn't in my right mind" when someone describes how they felt or acted when they received devastating news—because they truly weren't! That's why it's advisable to *not* make any big decisions or issue any ultimatums, much as you might want to, in the heat of the moment. You're in a state of shock, and your brain and body need time to process the information so you are able to think clearly.

When you first found out about the infidelity, how shocked were you?

_____

_____

What were your physical reactions?

_____

_____

_____

IDENTIFYING ANGER

"Anger is not the opposite of love, for the opposite of love is indifference. To be angry is to care tremendously. It is a signal that your caring extends beyond polite conversation, and you are willing to risk a confrontation to share how you feel."

—Doris Moreland Jones

Despite its negative connotation, anger is sometimes the appropriate response to things that happen, especially when they are thoughtless, cruel, inconsiderate, or hurtful. Obviously, infidelity is one of those things—so anger, along with hurt and resentment, is a natural and expected reaction when you discover that your partner has been unfaithful. Give yourself permission to be angry!

HOW DID YOUR ANGER MADE YOU FEEL?

Circle the words that most resonate with you.

- Enraged
- Exasperated
- Furious
- Incensed

- Infuriated
- Mad
- Provoked
- Resentful

- Riled
- Wrathful

IT'S OKAY TO BE ANGRY—BUT NOT FOREVER

There are two common ways that anger appears in response to infidelity, as described below:

CONSTRUCTIVE ANGER. This is the kind of anger that spurs you on to take charge of the situation. You accept this feeling and know that the initial blaze of fury will eventually die down so that you can make informed, smart, rational decisions about your future. When you're feeling constructive anger, you tell yourself, "I'm going to take charge."

DESTRUCTIVE ANGER. This is the kind of anger that might end up with you emotionally and unwittingly hurting yourself, your children, other family members, or others in your life, especially if the anger is consuming you. In dealing with your anger, even when you've been very hurt, balance is critical—in your response, the level of that response, and its duration. If after an extended time you still feel the same anger as when the infidelity was first discovered, this destructive anger will certainly stunt your healing process if anger is prolonged.

How did you express your anger when you found out about the infidelity?

_____

_____

What happened after you expressed your anger?

_____

_____

_____

How long did the initial anger last?

_____

Are you still angry?   Yes ☐ No ☐

Sometimes anger can seep out in other ways, directed at different targets. Because you have been wronged, you may find yourself taking your frustrations out on those around you, rather than or in addition to the person creating the frustration. When anger is intense, it's not hard to misplace it.

Have you ever taken your anger and frustration out on your friends, kids, parents, or dog instead of the person responsible for it?

Can you describe the situation?

_____

_____

_____

How did you recognize that you were doing this?

_____

_____

_____

SHIFTING THE BLAME

People can be left upset and speechless with rage when *they* get the blame for the actual act of infidelity. Yes, it takes two, but it can be incredibly painful when *you* bear the brunt of your ex's excuses or blame. It's even worse if your partner insinuated that you were responsible for their actions—especially if you heard something such as "If you had been better at _____, I wouldn't have been unfaithful."

I've had clients describe this sort of response, and sometimes it was because the ex wanted to end the relationship but didn't have the ability (or courage) to sit down and state what they wanted. Their infidelity then created a situation in which they could feel justified if their soon-to-be ex got very angry. In other words, the partner who was unfaithful used their partner's anger about the infidelity to give them the excuse they wanted so they could leave the relationship.

Did this happen to you?   Yes ❏ No ❏

If so, write down what happened.

_____

_____

_____

How did you deal with it?

_____

_____

_____

RECOGNIZE PATTERNS—YOURS, YOUR FAMILY'S, AND YOUR EX'S

Our emotional patterns are formed during childhood, when our parents or caregivers had their own ways of dealing with their anger. Recognizing your patterns of behavior can help you understand where they're coming from and help you manage them now and in the future.

A typical example comes from my client Emmett. His father was perpetually angry, losing his temper at anything at all—someone who could be described as a rageaholic. His mother, on the other hand, shut down and chose the silent treatment. Both types of anger were equally punishing, and neither was healthy or productive. When his mother found out about her husband's infidelity, she incorporated both patterns. She screamed and shouted at her husband for days, then stopped talking to him for weeks.

How did your mother manage her anger? Describe what it was like for you growing up.

_____

_____

_____

_____

How did your father manage his anger? Describe what it was like for you growing up.

_____

_____

_____

_____

How do you usually express anger?

_____

_____

Is this your default response?   Yes ☐   No ☐

Describe more specifically what you do when you're angry.

_____

_____

_____

_____

Is this something you learned from your parents?   Yes ☐ No ☐

If you could change your default response when you're furious, what would you want to do instead? For example, if you tend to be quick to react, do you then wish you could take back what you said a minute later?

_____

_____

_____

How did your partner manage anger?

_____

_____

When you had fights with your partner, how did they usually play out? What was a typical fight like?

_____

_____

_____

_____

Were you able to resolve the situations you were fighting about?   Yes ☐ No ☐

If so, how did that happen?

_____

_____

DO YOU HAVE FANTASIES OF REVENGE?

One of the most infamous cinematic depictions of destructive anger and revenge was in the 1995 film *Waiting to Exhale*, when the betrayed Angela Bassett character empties the contents of her unfaithful husband's very large closet into the family car, lights a cigarette, and sets it on fire. Audiences cheered when she did that! It certainly was cathartic for her in the moment—and for anyone watching who may have been subject to infidelity and wished they could have done something similar. But unlike real life, the film didn't deal with the repercussions of this rage.

It's a typical coping mechanism to have fantasies of revenge, to think about what dastardly deeds you could do to punish your ex and make you feel a whole lot better. If your partner had an affair with someone who was married and that person's spouse didn't know about it, a common fantasy is to tell all to the spouse. Or to announce it at the office Christmas party. Go ahead and give yourself permission to *think* those thoughts, as they can be quite cathartic. Acting on them, of course, is *not* okay; it's not what you think, it's what you *do*—though it's only human nature to smile when you see a yard sale sign that says, "GETTING RID OF MY CHEATING WIFE'S STUFF."

A good choice would be to write down your fantasies and then read them out loud. This should help you realize how impossible it would be to act on them.

Daniel, a client of mine, was so steamed at his wife for her adultery that he told her mother at a family reunion, which was his way of punishing not just his wife but her whole family. He apologized afterward and felt terrible about it for a long time, but the damage was done. He told me he really wished he hadn't done that, as it hurt a lot of people and he had to live with the fallout.

And as tempting as it might be, do not snoop. It's so easy to go on social media and start digging, and your anger may increase if you are communicating in any way with your ex's friends to get info on what your ex is doing, and with whom. Disconnect on all social media platforms. Don't look for reasons to contact your ex's friends. You might grow even more angry, when what you really want to do is to calm down!

Have you done something out of anger that you really regret?   Yes ☐ No ☐

If so, explain it here.

_____

_____

What were you hoping you'd feel by doing this?

_____

_____

Do you think you'll do something like this again?

_____

_____

IDENTIFYING TRUST

"I'm not upset that you lied to me, I'm upset
that from now on I can't believe you."

—Friedrich Nietzsche

Infidelity is not just about the act. It's about the hundreds of lies told to protect the act. That's the issue. Making a commitment to someone you loved deeply and then having your trust betrayed is incredibly painful. It can create a cascade effect that can trigger all the other emotions you'll read about in this chapter.

Trust is the cornerstone foundation of every relationship. You trust your parents to give you what you need when you don't even know what that is. Trust is what you want from your employer, your friends, and other family members. In a committed relationship, trust is earned and built over time.

Yet to fully trust is hard even in the best of times. As we get older and understand how the world works, it is common for us to be less inclined to trust. And learning to trust again after betrayal is one of the hardest things to do.

In other words, betrayal can take a long time to get over. Your whole world just went upside down. You exchanged vows to be faithful, and those were broken. You thought your partner was happy to confide in *you*—not the new employee at work. You had money and were comfortable, yet suddenly you're responsible for debts you didn't even know about. Every bit of *your* sense and security is gone. What I've heard from clients is this: "I've put twenty years of my life into trusting you, and your infidelity makes me feel like it was nothing to you."

I've heard many other scenarios, too, such as the wife whose single friend saw the husband posting on a site for married men who wanted a sexual hookup. Often the husband in this situation will lie at first. That happened to my client Joanna. "That wasn't me!" her husband protested. "Joe, my buddy at work, put me on there as a joke. He thought it was funny and never dreamed it would get out of hand!"

"Okay," said Joanna, "call Joe right now. I want to talk to him." Not surprisingly, her husband didn't want to call Joe. And that was the end of their relationship.

HOW DID YOUR EX BETRAY YOUR TRUST?

Technology has made it easier for people to be unfaithful and dishonest. But it also allows those who've discovered betrayal to find evidence of what has happened. When you know what to look for, everything can come to light. One of my clients discovered this when she saw a receipt from the drugstore where her partner had purchased condoms. She was on birth control, so there was no need for him to buy them. Another client didn't realize she'd signed up for points with a time stamp for when they were used at restaurants, so she was surprised when she got a message that showed someone had had seven glasses of wine—and she never drank.

How, specifically, was your trust betrayed?

_____

_____

_____

What can be even more painful is if your partner was unfaithful, apologized, and asked for forgiveness, and the two of you rebuilt your relationship. And then your partner did it again.

Was your trust betrayed more than once?   *Yes* ☐ *No* ☐

What happened?

_____

_____

_____

WHY YOU ARE DEVASTATED

One reason infidelity is so painful is that your trust has been upended. Promises had been made, and those promises were broken. Often those promises were about a life together—when to have children, where to live, which house to buy, and much more. Maybe you were even going to compromise on some of them, yet before you even got there, you were cheated on. And that upset your plans for the future, so now these things will never happen.

Sometimes such promises were not discussed at length in your relationship, but you've told yourself they were real because you wanted to believe they would eventually happen. If so, you may have tried to convince yourself of the following:

- I thought he would change after we got married.
- I thought she'd want kids. I told her I wanted four kids, and she changed the subject.
- I thought he would move to the suburbs or closer to other family members.
- She said she'd stop drinking/taking drugs.
- We both wanted two children, but when we couldn't get pregnant, he wouldn't adopt—even though he'd said he would.
- She said she didn't mind that we have different religions, but she would never celebrate my family's holidays with me.

If there were promises made and promises broken, what were they?

_____

_____

_____

_____

Did you tell yourself that promises had been made when they actually hadn't been?
Yes ❑ *No* ❑

If so, what were they?

_____

_____

_____

_____

DESCRIBE HOW HAVING YOUR TRUST BROKEN MADE YOU FEEL

Circle the words that resonate with you.

- Betrayed
- Deceived
- Duped

- Hoodwinked
- Misinformed
- Misled

- Mortified
- Tricked
- Two-timed

WHAT'S THE DIFFERENCE BETWEEN PRIVACY AND SECRETS?

Privacy is something that is nobody else's business. In life, your personal privacy is essential. It really is okay to not share every little detail with your partner, especially about earlier experiences that you might not wish to remember. So it's fair to tell your partner how much money you make, but not necessary to tell them something you're embarrassed about.

Secrecy, on the other hand, is intentional hiding. Hiding tends to be motivated by shame and fear. You're worried about judgment, and you fear you might lose something by sharing the secret. This often happens in relationships, especially early on, when you don't want to divulge a particular secret for fear that your partner won't want to be with you or love you anymore. Or you fear that telling could sabotage the relationship if your partner reacts negatively. Or someone who thinks his wife is being unfaithful confides in a friend, seeking advice and asking the friend not to share the conversation with anyone. In this case, a private situation turns into a secret.

In a long-term relationship, secrets can lead to anger and frustration. Henry and his wife Samantha were having problems. Henry knew that his porn-watching had become an addiction and that it made Samantha uncomfortable and upset. She asked Henry a lot of questions about it—which is fair—and about what, exactly, he watched. Henry lied to her. He felt her detailed questioning was invasive. Since he already felt so much shame and humiliation, he told himself that it was one thing to simply say he knew he was addicted and had to do something about it (exposing his secret), but another to divulge what turned him on when he watched the porn. He feared Samantha wouldn't understand some of his desires.

RECOGNIZE YOUR PATTERNS

Trust is about safety. Ideally, you grew up with a feeling of emotional safety in your family of origin. The first time you would have been cognizant of a lack of trust is when someone important to you said they'd do something, you believed them, and then they didn't come through. When you're a child and your parents do this, it can be very hard to let down your guard and trust people as you grow older.

Lucia had a mother who made it clear that she didn't want to hear any bad news from Lucia. It was Mom's way or the highway, which made it clear that she didn't trust Lucia to make her own decisions. When Mom said, "How are you?" Lucia was perceptive enough to know that she didn't really want to know. So Lucia learned to keep her feelings to herself—which is very common—and for a long time she found it hard to fully believe any of the men she dated when they asked her, "How are you?"

Can you recall an earlier time in your life when your trust was broken? What happened?

_____

_____

_____

Were you given autonomy to be yourself and learn who you were?

_____

_____

_____

What is your default response to situations about trust?

_____

_____

Is that something you learned from your parents? Yes ☐ No ☐

How do you usually deal with trust issues now?

_____

_____

_____

_____

IDENTIFYING DEPRESSION

"It is okay to have depression, it is okay to have anxiety, and it is okay to have an adjustment disorder. We need to improve the conversation. We all have mental health in the same way we all have physical health."

—Prince Harry

Clinical depression is a serious mental health condition that can be chronic and can recur for years (and that is beyond the scope of this book). Circumstantial or situational depression, however, is triggered by a particular life event. It understandably arises after painful circumstances, such as infidelity, any other kind of loss, or difficult circumstances that might be out of your control (like getting a new boss who is unkind and judgmental, but you aren't in a position where you can easily quit). Over time, this can morph into clinical depression, which needs treatment by experienced medical professionals.

According to the National Institute of Mental Health, "If you have been experiencing some of the following signs and symptoms most of the day, nearly every day, for at least two weeks, you may be suffering from depression:

- Persistent sad, anxious, or "empty" mood
- Feelings of hopelessness, or pessimism

- Feelings of irritability, frustration, or restlessness
- Feelings of guilt, worthlessness, or helplessness
- Loss of interest or pleasure in hobbies and activities
- Decreased energy, fatigue, or feeling "slowed down"
- Difficulty concentrating, remembering, or making decisions
- Difficulty sleeping, early morning awakening, or oversleeping
- Changes in appetite or unplanned weight changes
- Thoughts of death or suicide, or suicide attempts
- Aches or pains, headaches, cramps, or digestive problems—with no clear physical cause, and they don't ease even with treatment
- Suicide attempts or thoughts of death or suicide

DESCRIBE HOW DEPRESSION MAKES YOU FEEL

Circle the words that resonate with you.

- Blue
- Dejected
- Despondent
- Disheartened

- Down
- Glum
- Low
- Miserable

- Sad
- Unhappy

RECOGNIZE YOUR PATTERNS

I don't think I've met anyone who hasn't gotten depressed and sad after something hurtful happened to them. It's not so much an issue of trust as it is an issue of loss. There's no timetable for when the sadness (or anger, or other strong emotions) induced by infidelity will lift. For some, it's not that long; for others, it can persist for years.

Think of a time when you had another devastating loss. Perhaps it was the death of your grandmother, to whom you were very close, or an injury that prevented you from doing something you love.

Is the depression you're experiencing because of infidelity similar to any previous depression you've had? Yes ☐ No ☐

If so, how did you deal with depression then?

_____

_____

How do you usually deal with depression—what is your default response?

_____

_____

_____

Is that something you learned from your parents?   Yes ☐ No ☐

WHAT TO DO WHEN YOU'RE DEPRESSED

While depression is common after infidelity, that doesn't mean you should expect to needlessly suffer. These suggestions can help:

THERAPY. One-on-one or group therapy can be immensely helpful and give you a safe place to share your feelings. If your depression worsens, ask your physician about antidepressants that may help.

KEEPING IN TOUCH. This is the time to share how you feel with your friends. One of the most important things you can do is to not isolate yourself. It's not hard to lose perspective when you're on your own.

STAYING ACTIVE. If you're up to it, continue to do the things you love—dance classes or other hobbies, for instance—anything that will make you feel better.

SELF-SOOTHING TECHNIQUES. Mind and body-calming practices such as meditation, yoga, controlled breathing, and journaling (like this one!) can be very therapeutic.

SLOWING DOWN. Postpone important decisions, if possible.

***

In addition, according to the National Institute of Mental Health, you should:

- Try to get some physical activity. Just minutes of walking every day can boost one's mood.

- Try to maintain regular bedtime and wake-up times.

- Eat regular, healthy meals.

- Avoid using alcohol, nicotine, or drugs, including medications not prescribed for you.

- Do what you can as you can. Decide what must get done and what can wait.[2]

What are you doing to manage your depression?

_____

_____

_____

IDENTIFYING ANXIETY

"I am exhausted from trying to be stronger than I feel."

—Unknown

Like depression, serious anxiety—or generalized anxiety disorder—can persist for a very long time. Being anxious after infidelity is also situational and extremely common, especially if a person's life circumstances have changed in any way. Having to worry about paying the bills or finding childcare can make even the calmest people wring their hands and wonder what to do.

According to the National Institute of Mental Health, symptoms of generalized anxiety disorder (GAD) include the following:

- Feeling restless, wound-up, or on edge

- Being easily fatigued

- Having difficulty concentrating

- Being irritable

- Having headaches, muscle aches, stomachaches, or unexplained pains

- Having difficulty controlling feelings of worry

- Experiencing sleep problems, such as difficulty falling or staying asleep[3]

---

2 "Depression," National Institute of Mental Health, last modified April 2023, https://www.nimh.nih.gov/health/topics/depression.

3 "Generalized Anxiety Disorder: When Worry Gets Out of Control," National Institute of Mental Health, last modified 2022, https://www.nimh.nih.gov/health/publications/generalized-anxiety-disorder-gad.

Anxiety might also trigger panic attacks, which can be frightening. This is when you suddenly become intensely fearful and feel as if you're losing control, or that doom is on the horizon even when nothing is happening to trigger your fear. Because the response to a panic attack can be intense—heart racing and/or chest pain, ragged breathing, trembling or tingling, sweating or cold chills—many sufferers end up in the emergency room, as they are literally having the symptoms of a heart attack.

CASE STUDY: THE STRESS OF INFIDELITY

Let's take a look at the situation in which my clients Tonya and Nicole, both in their early thirties, found themselves. Tonya thought they had a solid and happy relationship. After five years together, though, Nicole started secretly texting an ex-girlfriend. After several months, they met up again. One thing led to another, and an affair ensued. Nicole felt so guilty about cheating on her partner that she ended up having a severe panic attack.

When she was sitting with Tonya in the emergency room, certain she was having a heart attack, she confessed to everything. Needless to say, this became an incredibly stressful and heartbreaking evening for both of them. In fact, it was so stressful that Tonya ended up having a panic attack a week later, but she recognized the symptoms and was able to calm herself without medical intervention. They tried to repair their relationship and went to couples therapy, but Tonya could not see herself trusting Nicole again. The sexual and emotional infidelity were deal-breakers. Because she couldn't see a future in which this betrayal wouldn't be consuming her, they split up for good.

DESCRIBE HOW ANXIETY MADE YOU FEEL

Circle the words that resonate with you.

- Apprehensive
- Concerned
- Fearful

- Fretful
- Frightened
- Panicked

- Uneasy
- Worried

According to the Mayo Clinic, post-traumatic stress disorder (PTSD) is "a mental health condition that's triggered by a terrifying event—either experiencing it or witnessing it. Symptoms may include flashbacks, nightmares, and severe anxiety, as well as uncontrollable thoughts about the event."[4] A formal diagnosis is given if symptoms persist for more than a month.

Because discovering infidelity is traumatic, it is possible to develop PTSD months or years later when something triggers the memory of that trauma. If, for example, you walked in on your partner in bed with someone else, it is understandable if you have flashbacks to that deeply upsetting moment. (Those with recurrent trauma should seek professional help.)

RECOGNIZE YOUR PATTERNS

Hopefully your anxiety will diminish as time goes on, and you will use your emotional skills to manage your new life. Being able to cope with infidelity-caused anxiety will serve you well in the future for any other difficult circumstances that might arise.

Is the anxiety you're experiencing now similar to any previous anxiety you've had?
Yes ☐ *No* ☐

If so, how did you deal with it then?

_____

_____

_____

What is your usual default response to anxiety?

_____

_____

_____

Is that something you learned from your parents?   *Yes* ☐ *No* ☐

---

4 "Post-Traumatic Stress Disorder (PTSD)," Mayo Clinic, last modified December 13, 2023, https://www.mayo clinic.org/diseases-conditions/post-traumatic-stress-disorder/symptoms-causes/syc-20355967.

ABOUT PERSEVERATION

When it comes to human behavior, I think the best way to describe "perseveration" is that it's when you get "stuck" on a certain topic. Infidelity and the end of a relationship—especially when you first find out—often create an endless loop of self-blame starting at the same point: *How could they do this to me? Why did they do this? What does that other person have that I don't? Why didn't I know? What will people think of me? Are they going to be disappointed in me? How am I going to face them? What did I do wrong?* And then it's back to, *How could they do this to me? Why did they do this?*

We've all been there—perseverating about a certain topic or situation that is upsetting or just drives us nuts. It's like mental hand-wringing that goes on and on and on. Occasionally I've had clients still talking about things that happened decades before, because they haven't been able to let go. Or they blame themselves for infidelity when it was their partner who cheated. Here's how this particular loop might sound: *If only I had lost those ten pounds that he hated, he would have found me more attractive, and he wouldn't have cheated. Oh why, oh why didn't I lose the weight?* When this happens, it's because we're caught up in the externals instead of asking ourselves why we keep going back to things that were clearly out of our control.

Breaking the perseveration loop isn't easy. You might not want to believe this, but many people who are perseverating have absolutely no idea that they're doing so. It's as if the same song is playing over and over, but they literally can't hear it! So it's important for you to recognize this behavior and to challenge it in order to make it go away. It's almost like talking yourself down from that obsessional ledge. Once you do, though, the perseverating will pass. These tips should help:

- Do something physical to shake yourself out of it. Give your body a jolt. Go for a quick walk around the block. Do twenty jumping jacks.

- Concentrate on deep, controlled breathing. Count out loud as you inhale and exhale. This will not only slow down your heart rate but reduce the adrenaline so that you'll feel calmer.

- Try listening to loud music for a few minutes to help drown out the repetitive loop in your brain.

- Ask friends to help. If you're still in the throes of it, you could be at an Italian restaurant and your friends are talking about the pasta, and you find yourself saying, "Oh, my ex loved puttanesca, and he got it every time we went out, and he ate this and ate that…." And you're off! Your friends know you have to get the ex-talk out of your system, but there's a limit. When friends tell you to stop, listen to them. They're on your side. You don't want to burn out your support network!

WHAT TO DO WHEN YOU'RE ANXIOUS

There are many ways to treat anxiety, and there is no reason to needlessly suffer. All the suggestions for treating depression on page 40 are applicable for anxiety as well.

What are you doing to manage your anxiety?

_____

_____

_____

_____

IDENTIFYING GRIEF AND SADNESS

"You cannot protect yourself from sadness without protecting yourself from happiness."

—Jonathan Safran Foer

Grief is the deep distress you feel after a devastating loss. Like depression and anxiety, it is a typical response to infidelity, as you mourn the betrayal of your trust and the end of your relationship.

THE DIFFERENT STAGES OF GRIEF

The end of any loving relationship is similar to dying and death—except that the person who betrayed you is still alive.

Grieving over infidelity creates a different kind of anger and sadness than grieving over the death of a loved one. The first stage will be acute pain, disbelief, anger—all the super-heated emotions you've already confronted in this chapter. The perspective of time helps grief take a different shape. Gradually these feelings will cool down somewhat and devolve into a still palpable but more manageable grief. It's not a linear process. You can feel sad and depressed and not feel that white hot anger any longer, and then something triggers your anger and it comes roaring back, and you're grieving all over again. Please don't beat yourself up if that happens—it is a common reaction to trauma.

In addition, both stages of grief are unique to *you*, and both will change over time. There's no way to quantify this, because everyone's situation is different. A person who is twenty-four and has been married for two years might not grieve as long as someone who's been married for seventeen years and has three children, which means there will always be a permanent reminder of the betrayal. The grief can be extreme in cases where a woman wanted desperately to have a baby, her partner hemmed and hawed about it, then cheated…and his girlfriend quickly became pregnant. That can hurt like hell for a long time.

For some people, grieving and sadness persist. No one can know what the future might bring, but the hurt isn't yet past. Some people never fall in love again, and they live with the painful memories every day. In some cases, grief turns to gratitude, especially if you fall in love again and have a better relationship (and even children) and a wonderful new life—one that never would have happened had your partner not been unfaithful. This doesn't change what happened, but it allows you to embrace your newfound happiness and hopes for the future.

DESCRIBE HOW GRIEF MADE YOU FEEL

Circle the words that resonate with you.

- Anguished
- Broken-hearted
- Despairing
- Devastated

- Distraught
- Distressed
- Grief-stricken
- Heartbroken

- Inconsolable
- Tearful
- Traumatized
- Weeping

RECOGNIZE YOUR PATTERNS

Is the grief you're experiencing now similar to any previous grief?   Yes ☐ No ☐

If so, how did you deal with it then?

_____

_____

_____

Is that something you learned from your parents?   Yes ☐ No ☐

WHAT TO DO WHEN YOU'RE GRIEVING

Time is your friend when it comes to grief. The acute stage might pass quickly or slowly. As your grief moves on over time, these tips should help:

- Be kind to yourself. Don't beat yourself up for feeling bad. You are mourning a great loss.

- If you want to have a pity party, you're entitled! But set a realistic time limit. Even the most satisfying parties have to come to an end at some point.

- Find supportive friends. Find support groups in person or online.

- Try not to say "I'm fine" when you really aren't. Ask for help when you need to.

- Don't become a hermit. At some point you'll have to pull off the covers and deal with reality. You were faced with infidelity, but that was then. This is now. You are now a survivor.

How long did the acute stage of your grief last?

_____

How did you feel during this time? Were there any physical symptoms, such as insomnia or inability to eat?

_____

_____

_____

_____

How are you managing your cooling-down grief? What are you doing to help yourself feel better?

_____

_____

_____

_____

IDENTIFYING STRENGTH AND COURAGE

"You never know how strong you are, until being strong is your only choice."

—Bob Marley

Now that you've dealt with all the tough stuff in this chapter, I want to leave you on a positive note. You deserve some kudos!

Dealing with monumental changes is difficult for everyone, and it's even harder when infidelity is the reason for those changes. Acknowledging your pain, confronting it head-on, and moving forward takes real strength and real courage.

"My wife cheated on me when our kids were little, and when we got divorced and I had to share custody and deal with everything being all messed up—when I was nursing a horrifically broken heart—I didn't see myself as brave," Henry told me. "My friends kept telling me I was, but all I could think of was how humiliated I was. I kept wondering what everyone was thinking about me, and what a fool I'd been to not notice what was going on. I was harder on myself than anyone else was—and I certainly didn't want their pity. But eventually I started to believe that my friends were right. I was brave. Staying level-headed did take courage. Now, I can look back on all the ups and downs of my emotions and realize I came through to the other side where I am stronger, smarter, and ready for whatever happens next."

Do you see yourself as strong or courageous?   Yes ☐ No ☐

If not, why not?

_____

_____

_____

_____

_____

List all the examples of your strength and courage that you can think of. You've got this!

_____

_____

_____

_____

_____

CHAPTER 3

NEW CIRCUMSTANCES AND A CHANGED LIFESTYLE

"We cannot choose our external circumstances, but we can always choose how we respond to them."

—Epictetus

What happens to your lifestyle when the relationship ends?

Even if your relationship had been troubled for some time and you're actually relieved to be able to move on to the next phase of your life, repercussions to your lifestyle are inevitable. Infidelity changes you!

One of the hardest things to deal with beyond the initial shock of betrayal is knowing that your life is going to be different. What are you going to do? What do you tackle first? How are you going to cope? How are you going to *live*?

There might be drastic changes, such as immediate financial problems. What if your partner paid all the bills and did all the paperwork? Do you even know the passwords needed to make online payments?

And then there are the little daily things that accumulate over time and that you're really going to miss—or that hopefully you be thrilled to get out of your life (good riddance to your partner wearing that stained college tee shirt, full of holes, all weekend!). Add to the mix the emotional drain of having to put up a brave front. You can be utterly exhausted by the thought of sitting next to each other at your daughter's little league games, but you need to navigate these feelings, so they don't spill toward your child's experience of the situation.

IDENTIFY YOUR LOSSES AND LIFESTYLE CHANGES

I've compiled a list of the most common issues that clients have discussed with me. Take your time going through this list, as it will help you identify situations you might not have thought of before. It will also help you renegotiate with yourself about what has changed, what will stay the same, and what's worth fighting over—or isn't.

Check off each item that resonates with you, then add your own experiences at the end of each section.

FINANCES

See Chapter 6 for much more on this topic.

- [ ] If you are getting divorced, where is the money coming from to pay for the legal counsel you need?
- [ ] How are the bills to be paid?
- [ ] Where are all the passwords for every account?
- [ ] How are expenses being vetted once your partner moves out and you still have a joint account?
- [ ] Who owns the home and is listed on the deed, or who signed the lease?
- [ ] If you have a lease, who gets the security deposit back if you move out?

SOCIAL LIFE

See Chapter 7 for more on this topic.

- [ ] What are some things you did as a couple?
- [ ] Who gets the friends?
- [ ] Who gets the therapist you both saw?

THE CHILDREN

- [ ] Who gets custody?
- [ ] Who deals with and pays for child care, if needed?

- ☐ Who pays for items the children need, such as clothing and accessories?
- ☐ Who pays the school expenses?
- ☐ Which parent does the teacher call when there's a problem at school? Is it the schools' responsibility to call one or both parents?
- ☐ Who will be the legal guardians specified in your will?

What change hit you the hardest at first?

_____

_____

_____

What change still hits you hard? Why?

_____

_____

_____

What do you still miss? Why do you think you miss it so much?

_____

_____

_____

DEALING WITH POSSESSIONS

Deciding who gets what is a difficult task, as even the smallest objects can trigger painful memories of when you were in love and happy together. It's really okay to mourn the loss of even small things (like the pressed flower from your first date, or the joke coffee cup he got you on your fourth anniversary). Often there will be things you want to hold on to because if your ex takes them, a part of you goes with them. Keeping photographs of what you used to have just isn't the same.

"I can't believe my ex took my old TV," Joy said to me. "It was small and shaped sort of like a spaceship, and I got it as a present for my high school graduation—it wasn't his to take! His excuse was that he liked it better than I did, but of course he never asked me, so how would he know?"

You might be happy to get rid of some of your partner's possessions that you never cared for, or you might be devastated at wrangling over the dog or cat. (This is a big one, as pets are beloved family members. If you have children, a good compromise is that the pet goes wherever the kids go if there's shared custody, or you compromise on shared custody of the pet if it's logistically feasible; if one person moves hundreds of miles away, that's a problem. And then you have to figure out who pays for the vet.)

Bear in mind that dealing with joint possessions is going to be even more difficult when you're feeling angry and hurt. If your partner left your home after you broke up, you're still living in a place suffused with shared memories and belongings. If you are the one who left, you're dealing with adjusting to a new home, and that's never easy in the best of circumstances. Neither of you should just take things without permission, although people often do—leading to more conflicts.

Possessions aren't always tangible items that you can put your hands on, as you'll see in the following list. Some of them can be pricey, not just when you bought them but when you must replace them. Add your own inventory to the end of this list.

ITEM	ME	MY EX
Airline miles	☐	☐
Artwork	☐	☐
Cars	☐	☐
Cleaning equipment	☐	☐
Clothing/accessories you both wore	☐	☐
Dual/family membership at the gym	☐	☐
Expensive items, such as antiques or objects d'art	☐	☐
Furniture	☐	☐
Household goods	☐	☐

ITEM	ME	MY EX
Netflix and other streaming accounts	☐	☐
Pets	☐	☐
Photographs	☐	☐
Rugs	☐	☐
Season tickets (sporting events, theater, concerts, etc.)	☐	☐
Sporting equipment	☐	☐
Storage unit (Do you even know what's in there?)	☐	☐
Subscriptions	☐	☐
Tools	☐	☐
Weeks at a time-share or vacation club	☐	☐
	☐	☐
	☐	☐
	☐	☐
	☐	☐

What possession(s) did you lose that you still want and are upset about?

_____

_____

Why do you still want that possession?

_____

_____

Precisely what do you most miss about it?

_____

_____

What possession(s) don't you miss? Why not?

_____

_____

_____

TIPS ON DIVIDING THE SPOILS

I've heard plenty of stories about couples who fought so much and for so long over divvying up the possessions that their lawyers ended up getting paid far more than the possessions were ever worth. Even couples who start out with the best of intentions can quickly morph from calm and collected to "Are you freaking kidding me? No way can you have that!"

These tips should help when you're trying to divide shared possessions with your ex:

- If you're still living in the home you shared with your ex, take a detailed inventory of all the possessions. Do so in writing, and take photos. Share this with your ex. The process can be painful and triggering, so you might want to ask a friend to help you. A friend could also help speed up the process.

- Send the inventory to your ex via email. This allows you to discuss it online without having to face each other in person.

- Don't have discussions about possessions with your ex when you're hungry, tired, or very stressed. It will be harder to stay calm and rational in that state.

- If your ex is coming over to pick things up, have a friend with you to be a referee of sorts if you feel you need it, as you might be so angry and upset that you unintentionally start a fight. Allow yourself to admit that this is going to be painful and emotional. This is probably not the time to express all the things you've been saving up to say—even if your ex deserves it. Ask yourself in advance if you'd feel bad about a confrontation a few weeks or months from now. Going for the jugular might temporarily give you some relief, or it might not. Your friend can be a silent supporter, not a chance to gang up on your ex, as deserved as that might be. And try not to punch the wall in frustration afterward!

- You have a full claim to anything that belonged to you before this relationship began, just as your ex does with their things. Make a list of your must-have items and what you are willing to negotiate about.

- Pick your battles. Be strategic about how you divvy up items. If you'd be thrilled to get rid of your ex's favorite chair but they think you love it, graciously offer it to them. Saying goodbye to something you don't care about is a lot easier than giving up something you cherish.

- Sometimes, fortunately, getting rid of shared things can be unexpectedly positive. Take my client Marcus. "My ex and I fought and fought over a contemporary oil painting, and a few months later I realized it was no longer a fight I needed to win. The truth was, I didn't really want the painting; it was actually a reminder of what had become an unhappy relationship finished off by my ex's infidelity. And what was amazing about this whole situation was that this painting was a portrait of a person who looked a lot like me, but of course it wasn't me. So one day I went to my ex's apartment building and just left the painting with the doorman. My ex got stuck with a portrait that was a daily reminder of the person he'd betrayed. It was very satisfying to get it out of the house."

Are you holding on to something because you just don't want your ex to have it—not because you really want or need it? Are you trying to protect your possession or trying to control everything because you're angry? (These are tough questions, necessitating self-examination about your anger.)

_____

_____

_____

_____

Why are your must-keep items important to you?

_____

_____

What are you really holding on to?

_____

_____

_____

List the things your ex surprisingly said you could keep, or that you thought there'd be a fight over but there wasn't.

_____ _____

_____ _____

_____ _____

_____ _____

List all the things you're glad to get rid of!

_____ _____

_____ _____

_____ _____

_____ _____

Do you feel better about having fewer possessions?   Yes ☐ No ☐

If so, why?

_____

_____

_____

Do you feel worse?   Yes ☐ No ☐

If so, why?

_____

_____

_____

WHY DO SO MANY WOMEN CUT THEIR HAIR AFTER A BREAKUP?

"I'm Gonna Wash That Man Right Outa My Hair" is a famous song from the 1949 musical *South Pacific*. It still resonates today, because so many people feel an intense urge to cut their hair after a relationship ends. It's a highly visible sign of a new you, a new start. It's who you are now, not who you used to be—because you're not that person anymore!

Getting a new hairstyle is also far easier than making changes to your body (such as losing weight or starting a new fitness regimen), which can take weeks if not months to show tangible results. And, if your partner always wanted you to do your hair a certain way to please them more than it pleased you, changing your hairstyle after a breakup can make you feel a whole lot better.

If you're tempted to cut or color your hair, though, it might be best to wait until after the initial shock of infidelity or the relationship's end has worn off. Hair will always grow back, but a few days later you might not be happy with the buzz cut the hair stylist encouraged you to get!

THE FEAR OF LONELINESS

"I'd rather be miserable with you than without you," Gigi says to her true love, Gaston, at the end of the movie *Gigi*.

That's a provocative and unfortunately all-too-relatable line. Many unhappy couples stay together because they just don't want to be alone. And this is completely understandable. People tend to leave their relationships only after being unfaithful because they know they have someone else to go to. They just can't deal with the thought of living on their own.

This is what Mary did. She wanted to end her relationship, as she knew it was no longer healthy, but she wasn't willing to give it up yet. She wanted a soft landing before she'd leave (though that can backfire—Mary was now keeping her own secrets). She hung on for a year after her husband George was unfaithful because she didn't want to be alone. They were supposedly working on improving their relationship, but Mary knew deep down that she'd never be able to trust him again. And all the signs were there that George was still seeing his girlfriend. She surprised herself when she met someone she really liked, and when that relationship seemed to have genuine possibilities, she filed for divorce. In a surprise twist, George's girlfriend also broke up with him, as she got fed up with his endless promises to leave Mary; she couldn't trust him, either!

There is, of course, a vast difference between being alone (which can be emotionally satisfying) and being lonely (which is not). Some of the loneliest people I've ever met are couples who no longer feel comfortable with any kind of intimate behavior, yet they don't know what to do about it. Your partner can be sitting next to you on the sofa, yet there is nothing about their presence that makes you feel cherished or supported. If this is the case, it can be a relief when the relationship ends.

There can also be hidden triggers for loneliness after a relationship ends. Seeing the closet and dresser drawers and garage empty can give you a huge jolt that leaves you feeling sad and lonely. When all that's left are particles of dust where the shoes had been, or you find a fortune from a fortune cookie you ate on your honeymoon stuck in between drawers, it can feel like you've been stabbed in the heart all over again. Unexpected triggers can also sneak up on you. For example, if you had your partner as your emergency contact number—for your bank, work, schools, even when booking an airline ticket—and you suddenly realize this must change. Who will you list instead?

Social media doesn't help with loneliness, either. We've become a nation of texters, and while it's nice to get a lot of messages on your phone, that's just not the same as talking to or seeing a person in the flesh. The pandemic certainly showed us that. Although social media can keep you busy, physically seeing others can shift your mood, and the sound of the human voice is really important. How often does your phone ring? If it does, is it a real person that you know or spam?

And the sound of silence in the house can be deafening.

There are many things to miss when a relationship ends, and they can make you feel lonely. Doing anything on the following list on your own, especially soon after your relationship has ended, can be very, very difficult—particularly if your ex had been helpful with chores and fixing things, dealt with computer issues, or made coffee for you every morning. But the more you do things on your own, the less jarring it will feel over time. I know people who now love going to the movies or eating out on their own. They find it empowering, and it's an excellent way to realize that strangers really do not care and aren't judging you for being on your own.

What about being a couple do you miss, making you feel lonely in any way? Check off those that apply to you.

❒ You knew your partner would come home at night and you'd have someone to talk with about nothing in particular, and a warm body in your bed.

❒ You had someone to be with over the holidays, especially New Year's Eve.

❒ You had more plans with friends and family when your partner's social circle was added to yours.

❒ When your partner went out with friends, you relished that time on your own—but there's no longer anyone you're automatically going to be with when you don't have plans.

❒ You didn't feel the need to do anything, because you knew you had company.

❒ You had a travel companion, a restaurant companion, and a companion for going to the movies, the theater, concerts, or sporting events. And if you traveled, you had someone to drop you off and pick you up at the airport.

❒ You had someone to help with cooking, shopping, and chores around the house.

❒ You didn't worry so much about your personal safety, as your partner was in the house with you and would check up on you if you were late coming home.

Add your own situations to the following list.

_____

_____

_____

_____

_____

_____

What do you miss the most about being a couple?

_____

_____

_____

_____

_____

_____

_____

What makes you the loneliest? List as much as you need to.

_____

_____

_____

_____

_____

_____

_____

_____

_____

FIGHTING THE LONELINESS

If you're feeling lonely, try to take steps to make yourself feel better. The longer you avoid doing anything proactive, the longer it can take to not feel so alone. Loneliness should not be discounted—it's practically an epidemic in this country, and it can have serious health effects. In fact, in 2023 the National Institute on Aging released a study showing that the health risks of being isolated for a lengthy period of time are equivalent to smoking fifteen cigarettes a day.[5]

To start, do something for yourself. Tell yourself "I deserve this"—because you do! And sometimes the best thing is to do something for someone else. Redirecting your attention to something out of your range of experience—whether it's volunteering at an animal shelter or a hospital, or any kind of volunteering that brings you into contact with other people—will feel good. And don't forget to set up regular check-ins with your friends.

What can you do or are currently doing for others to help you feel less lonely?

_____

_____

_____

_____

_____

_____

WHAT YOU *WON'T* MISS IN THE FUTURE

When you've been involved with and loved someone for any extended period of time, there will always be things about them that drove you crazy.

Everyone does things that annoy their partner. That's life with someone else! Maybe you didn't realize how grating these things were at first, but over time they bugged the heck

---

5 "Social isolation, loneliness in older people pose health risks," National Institute on Aging, last modified April 23, 2019, https://www.nia.nih.gov/news/social-isolation-loneliness-older-people-pose-health-risks.

out of you—and you're absolutely not going to miss them. Maybe those things were petty, or they might have been unhygienic enough to put your health at risk. Of course, this doesn't mean that the next person in your life isn't going to do all those same things, but I hope you can laugh about some of what you'll put on your list. That will help take the sting out of the pain you might be feeling.

The passage of time and a new perspective can make you realize that you weren't getting your emotional needs met in the way you'd hoped. Often, people don't realize that the reason their needs weren't met was because they weren't being heard. You certainly won't miss talking into the void when what you had wanted was a loving partner who listened to you. This will be discussed in more detail in Chapter 9.

It can help to notice what is actually better now that your relationship is over. For example, you won't have to deal with some of the following things anymore. Add as many things to this list as you like!

Will you really miss…?

- The toilet seat left up (or down)
- The noise of video games played until three in the morning (and then being lied to about it)
- Your ex calling their mother three times a day to complain about everything
- Annoying or unsupportive in-laws
- Your ex's annoying or intrusive friends and colleagues
- Fighting about politics
- Not being able to spend more time with your own friends or relatives because your ex thought theirs were more important
- Your ex rearranging condiments in the pantry—when they never cooked
- Your ex always taking the last cookie
- Endless sporting events playing on the TV
- Going to the ballet when you never liked it
- Poor hygienic habits (don't get me started!)
- The toilet paper being replaced the wrong way
- Constantly being interrupted

- Whining about doing household chores
- Getting promises that something will be done but then it isn't, and you're accused of being a nag
- Never getting anywhere on time because your ex couldn't be bothered
- Having to repeat yourself because they hadn't listened in the first place
- Having to pretend to like their friends
- The endless fights
- Feeling like you're stuck
- Knowing in your heart that this relationship cannot be fixed

_____

_____

_____

_____

_____

_____

_____

PART II

HEALING FROM INFIDELITY— STRATEGIES THAT WORK

"What I learned was how easy it is to be blinded by your own desire to deceive yourself."

—Emma Thompson

CHAPTER 4
SEXUAL INFIDELITY

"Infidelity is a deal breaker for me. I've broken up with people
over it. You can't do monogamy 90 percent of the time."

—Alanis Morissette

In this world there are breakups and *breakups*. Couples often split up when there's no infidelity—the relationship just didn't work. Yes, the breakup was a terrible experience. But if you're healthy and in charge of yourself and have no children tying you to your ex, while you're likely disappointed and sad for the loss of your fantasy about what could have been, you know you can move on with your life.

When sexual infidelity has happened to you, though, that's a *breakup*.

Sex is a life force. It's something that connects people, moving them in what can be the most wonderful way beyond friendship and into true intimacy. Its intensity can make you feel exhilaration both emotionally and physically. And, of course, it's not just about the physical act itself but about the closeness and the comfort of the moments before and after. This is why newly formed sexual relationships can be glorified—the feelings released are *that* powerful.

But when you find out that there has been sexual betrayal from someone you wholly trusted and loved deeply, the feelings this engenders are going to be equally intense.

Sex is something we think about and/or experience regularly, but many people are uncomfortable talking about it. I do think it's more common for women to talk candidly to their friends about their sex lives, while men may be loath to bring it up—especially if there are performance or dysfunction problems. Sometimes people are just embarrassed to bring it up because they think they should already know the answers, or they were raised to think sex is too private to share. No one wants to be judged by their sexual experiences or lack thereof.

After decades of counseling experience, I know that it is especially difficult for people to talk about sex during therapy with their partner present. There's shame. There's embarrassment. There's disappointment. There's fear of being judged. There's a sense of failure.

As a result, it can be months before a client will broach the topic of finding out that their ex had had sex with another person, and the profound pain of betrayal that followed. Instead, they'll talk about anything else going on in their lives, though I can often tell that something is wrong. Sometimes a client will simply shrug and tell me it's not that important, saying something like, "I've been married for over a dozen years and we're just having a bad patch." Sometimes they don't tell me until years later! Sometimes I have an understanding about what might be going on because both members of a couple will be silent on the subject. Just recently I asked a couple about intimacy, and both responded in unison—"Fine." Hopefully they'll come to the point where they simply can't hold it in any longer and the truth will be revealed.

If you can't have that conversation with anyone, the pages of this workbook are here for you.

YOUR SEX LIFE BEFORE SEXUAL INFIDELITY

Because you will be moving on from the relationship that has caused you so much pain, it can be very helpful—although it might be a bit difficult—to sit down with yourself and have an honest conversation about the sexual relationship you had with your ex. Be as truthful as you can about your sexual needs and desires. Sexual desire is a normal part of the human experience. This will allow you to pinpoint what worked and what didn't, what you like and what you don't, and it will help you find your voice so you can identify and speak up about these feelings and desires in the future.

Answer the following questions about your sex life in the months or years leading up to the infidelity in your marriage. People in the throes of new love, at the beginning of what turns into a long-term relationship, tend to have an active and passionate sex life, falling into bed several times a week (or more). And then this tends to slow down when life—work pressures, children, finances, health issues—gets in the way.

What was your sex life like after the initial intensity of your relationship settled down?

_____

_____

_____

What was best about your sex life with your ex?

_____

_____

_____

What didn't you like?

_____

_____

_____

Did you ever fake an orgasm? If so, why?

_____

_____

Were you totally honest with your ex about your needs and desires?

_____

_____

_____

How did your sexual needs and behavior change over time? Be brutally honest here, because if your needs diminished over time while your partner's didn't, that may have influenced your relationship.

_____

_____

_____

_____

THE **COURAGE** TO **WALK AWAY**

Did your ex want things you weren't comfortable with? If so, were you able to say what you actually wanted or needed?

_____

_____

_____

Was role play important for either of you? If so, did it please you?

_____

_____

_____

Was one person more dominant in expectations than the other?   Yes ☐ No ☐

Was porn a problem? If so, how?

_____

_____

_____

YOUR RESPONSE TO SEXUAL INFIDELITY

HOW DID SEXUAL INFIDELITY MAKE YOU FEEL?

There are countless reasons why people are unfaithful to someone they love. But the reaction of the partner in response is nearly always the same. Shock comes first, followed by disbelief and/or denial that this could be happening to you. Followed by rage. Sometimes followed by resignation. Followed by well-founded worries about the repercussions—emotional (your trust upended), financial (what this might mean for your future), and physical. (If your ex was intimate with you and someone else at the same time, were you at risk for any sexually transmitted diseases? Was there a feeling of revulsion that you'd been sharing your ex intimately with someone else?)

Once the initial shock and disbelief wears off, often it can take a months or longer to process everything. Perhaps there were suspicions that have now been confirmed and clarified—you're thinking back to things that were said or done that didn't quite make sense at the time. There might also be relief in finding that you weren't wrong to think something was amiss, and you can now deal with the truth rather than deception.

The excuses and "explanations" you might have heard are legion, as well as whom you heard them from. I had a client who got a phone call out of the blue from the mistress, announcing that she was pregnant; this was a double whammy of deception for the betrayed woman, who'd been trying to get pregnant herself. Some have found out about a workplace affair because their partner got fired. Sometimes the betrayer confesses. They might be feeling guilty or contrite or empowered and out the door—and the truth needs to come out. There's a famous *New Yorker* cartoon where a woman is standing in her bedroom, looking at her partner in bed with his lover, and he says, "It's not me."

Your feelings need to be validated. What's important to tell yourself is *why* the cheating matters, though you may never know all the reasons. And even if you did, you're past the point of needing to dissect motives. It doesn't matter how long or in what manner the sexual infidelity happened. It happened, you found out, you made your decision, and your relationship is over.

How did you discover the sexual infidelity?

_____

_____

_____

How did you confront your partner about it?

_____

_____

_____

What did your partner say in response?

_____

_____

_____

What was your own initial response?

_____

_____

What happened next?

_____

_____

How were you feeling a few days later?

_____

_____

A MILLION WAYS TO SNOOP

Let's be perfectly honest. We all snoop in many different arenas—checking phones, emails, or texts; investigating how often a partner watched porn; or opening mail not addressed to us. We want to see what's going on that has nothing to do with infidelity. A common snoop is looking at your partner's social media platforms and seeing whom they've interacted with or "liked" or commented on.

It's just human nature, and it's probably going to happen, but you know already that satisfying your curiosity once you found out about the sexual infidelity—especially if you're still very angry—is not going to end well. But you still want to investigate and find any evidence of betrayal that you missed or feel is important to ferret out. You can feel as if you've had to become a police detective checking on your own life, with forensic-level snooping.

Thanks to social media, smart phones, tracking devices, and the internet, it has become far easier to follow the trail of deception. Before we were connected online, people had to get out of their homes in order to betray their partners, and that meant there was always a risk that they would be seen and discovered. Now a person can sit in their living room, on their phone while everyone else is streaming a TV show, and give in to the temptation that is right there at their fingertips.

But it has also become much more challenging to be unfaithful; using technology to cheat often comes with an added layer of lying, because the betrayal has to be more devious in terms of finding someplace secret to meet and then hiding any receipts that could show up on shared credit card bills or apps.

Bear in mind, however, that when you snoop, you'll be opening up the rabbit hole and falling down into it. You find all sorts of things that, once seen, can't be unseen or unheard or unread. This rarely makes you feel better and can be incredibly painful, yet you can be so stunned by what you've seen or heard that it can be almost like driving by a car wreck—you don't want to look but you can't look away, either. Again, it is only human nature to try to understand why, even if the why might never be known—or it could be something that might hurt you even more when you learn the details.

For example, it is likely pretty easy to check your ex's social media accounts or other websites they may have visited. You might not be aware of a website called Ashley Madison, launched in 2001. Its motto? "Life is short, have an affair." This was a site set up for the sole purpose of allowing people to be unfaithful. At one point it had an astonishing 65 million members worldwide, and every one of them was outed when the site was hacked in 2015. Many of those who were exposed said they'd only gone on the site "out of curiosity," and that may well have been true…or it could have been an excuse. The site wouldn't have become so successful if the intent behind those 65 million hadn't been one of duplicity.

Going online to see if your ex was telling the truth about something—perhaps they told you they couldn't have the kids when they were supposed to because of a business trip, but then you see a photo of them out with the new partner—can morph into obsessive checking. Some of my clients have told me that they checked their ex's phone when they had a chance and deeply regretted it, as they saw passionate texts about sexual desire for someone else—and worse, graphic sexts. You might even have seen messages identical to what were sent to you early in your relationship; that once-fun behavior between the two of you is now shared with someone else. It is likely painful to see similar behavior shared with someone else—yet one more thing to turn the screws.

THE **COURAGE** TO **WALK AWAY**

Chronic snooping is often about looking for some sort of rationalization or validation that is unlikely to be given. If your ex is unfaithful with a much younger person who is a famous model, you can at least tell yourself that this was about physical desire. But if the person is less attractive (not just physically), it can make you wonder why you weren't "enough" for your ex. And if you see your ex with someone who has children or is pregnant with *their* baby—after being adamant with you about not wanting children—this can break your heart, making you feel misunderstood and unwanted. It's doubtful that you will see you ex saying, "Oh, I am so depressed because I cheated on my wife." Even if there are regrets, they're not the kind of thing you'll see on social media.

Have you snooped on your ex?   Yes ☐ No ☐

How many times a day?

_____

Exactly what did you do?

_____

_____

_____

If your ex has a new partner, do you check them out?   Yes ☐ No ☐

If so, what do you do?

_____

_____

Have you driven by where they live now or hung out near where they work in hopes of finding something or having an encounter?   Yes ☐ No ☐

Did you make plans with mutual friends to get information on your ex?
Yes ☐ No ☐

If so, what did you do?

_____

_____

How did doing any of the above make you feel?

_____

_____

_____

_____

Did you learn anything that was helpful or made you feel better?

_____

_____

_____

Was knowing the details you discovered better than not knowing?

_____

_____

_____

DID YOU FIND YOURSELF DOING THIS?

- Looking in your spouse's pockets
- Examining clothing for stains or smells
- Checking all credit card bills, including the business credit card
- Investigating the computer hard drive and/or thumb drives
- Seeing if any passwords have been changed
- Reading texts and/or direct messages on social media
- Checking the mileage on the car
- Looking on notepads or sticky notes because you might be able to see what had been written on the previous sheet
- Installing tracking apps
- Using "Find My Phone"

THE **COURAGE** TO **WALK AWAY**

WHAT ABOUT THE WHAT-IFS?

It's only human nature to go through the litany of what-ifs when you're dealing with betrayal. Yet the what-ifs can make how you feel much worse in so many ways.

One client was a brilliant woman who was at the top of her field, with a vibrant, engaging personality. Her husband left her for a younger, slimmer woman who worked in a clothing boutique and went to the gym five times a week. He needed somebody who looked a certain way to make himself feel better. Another client was a man whose wife was unfaithful with someone much younger as well, but in this case the husband was fifteen years older than his soon-to-be ex-wife. The age difference hadn't bothered her when they got married; it only did when people starting thinking he was her father.

I've found that the what-ifs are often about people beating themselves up because of their physicality:

- If the ex was unfaithful with someone younger, the what-if might be, "What if I'd tried harder to look more youthful?"

- If the ex was unfaithful with someone thinner or obviously fit and strong, it could be, "What if I'd lost more weight and worked out more?"

- If the ex was unfaithful with someone you knew, the what-if can be, "What if I'd been more like that person, with that kind of personality?"

Have you found yourself going down a mental rabbit hole of what-ifs? What's the first thing you say to yourself—and then find yourself in the weeds?

_____

_____

_____

If you go through a mental list of what-ifs, are there certain ones you get stuck on?

_____

_____

_____

SEXUAL INFIDELITY

Did your ex make negative comments about your body? If so, what were they?

_____

_____

About your education? If so, what were they?

_____

_____

About your job? If so, what were they?

_____

_____

About your family? If so, what were they?

_____

_____

About your friends? If so, what were they?

_____

_____

About your habits? If so, what were they?

_____

_____

Did you agree with those comments? How did you respond?

_____

_____

_____

DEALING WITH NEGATIVE SELF-TALK

Thinking about the what-ifs and other triggers can cause sadness and grief, leading to stress that can become overwhelming. Not only do you need to find as many ways as you can to make yourself feel better (see Strategies for Stress Relief on page 127), but you need to find a way to challenge the negative self-talk that can leave you sleepless at night and miserable during the day.

NEGATIVE SELF-TALK	POSITIVE REFRAMING
I made a mistake.	It's not the end of the world.
I had thought our marriage was great.	I have to admit, I wasn't always happy.
If only I hadn't....	I can't change the past.
I should have listened to them.	I should listen to myself.
Why didn't I	I had a good reason, and I don't doubt myself now.
I ruined everything.	It takes two people to ruin things.
What if I had stayed home more?	It wouldn't have made a difference.

REFRAMING THE WHAT-IFS

Sexual infidelity shakes you to your very core, and even things you didn't question before can now become endless questions. For instance, it is unfortunately more common than you might imagine that people are unfaithful with their partner's best friend, or with a relative. This upends not only your life but also that of your circle of friends or family. It also ties in to larger issues that we all have to deal with—ageism (Is the new person younger, and by how much?) and social media distortions of real life (Is the new person well known, with many followers?).

What can be immensely conflicting is this: When you wanted comfort and closeness, who could make you feel better than the one person who has now made you feel worse? And because sex is such a loaded topic, betrayal can engender a lot of feelings you might not feel comfortable talking out with anyone.

Remember, what *you* think about is what determines how *you* feel. What other people think might be intruding into the situation, and at the end of the day this is about keeping out the voices that aren't your own. You are the one who decides.

How has this experience with your ex changed the way you view yourself?

_____

_____

_____

In what way? Give an example.

_____

_____

_____

What have you learned?

_____

_____

_____

What person first comes to mind as someone whom you feel safe talking to?

_____

Are there certain triggers or things/places that you need to stay away from because you know you're going to feel bad or down on yourself if you don't? If so, list them here.

_____

_____

_____

Since you discovered the sexual infidelity, do you find that you're being critical not just of your partner but of yourself as well?   Yes ☐ No ☐

THE **COURAGE** TO **WALK AWAY**

Are there people you should stay away from because you know they're going to say, "I told you so?" Yes ☐ No ☐

Who are the people who support you without trashing your ex?

_____

_____

_____

Do you feel better after talking to your friends or not? Why?

_____

_____

_____

How would you describe how you feel now compared to how you felt when you initially found out about the infidelity?

_____

_____

_____

What has changed?

_____

_____

_____

CHAPTER 5

EMOTIONAL INFIDELITY

*"That was how dishonesty and betrayal started,
not in big lies but in small secrets."*

—Amy Tan

What is emotional infidelity? It's different from the undeniable and deliberate infidelity that's sexual or financial. If a person has sex with someone who's not their partner, that's undeniable. Or if someone isn't honest about how money is being spent, that's deliberate.

The stereotype is that women are looking for an emotional connection when seeking an affair, whereas men are more interested in the physical at first but over time may become emotionally linked. Yet this is not always true. Emotional infidelity can happen to anyone.

THE ROOTS OF EMOTIONAL INFIDELITY

Emotional infidelity can take weeks, months, or even years to develop. It often begins as a truly innocent friendship. Both parties can be taken by surprise at what then starts happening. Sometimes it's simply about who's there in the moment. There is often no physical attraction whatsoever; some people may remain in this situation for years and never touch each other physically. In many cases one person is in a committed relationship and has no desire for a sexual affair—but the two of them are still very, very connected.

Realizing that your partner has become emotionally intimate with someone else can be even more threatening and devastating than sexual infidelity. It's especially tricky when this happens due to a workplace relationship—what's commonly referred to as the "office wife" or "office husband" because that person is seen every day at work, usually for at least eight hours (as much time or more than your partner spends with you during your weekday waking hours). There's accessibility and availability without having to plan anything, as people need to do to keep sexual affairs secret.

80

THE **COURAGE** TO **WALK AWAY**

A common scenario in movies is when one partner is attracted to the nanny or housekeeper, who by the nature of their job is in the home. The home creates common interests, and a nanny who's always there will already have an emotional connection with the family because of the baby or children in their care. And who drives the babysitter home? It's almost always the dad!

It can be difficult or unfeasible for anyone to quit a job while in the midst of this kind of relationship, which compounds the problem—as you'll see with my clients Rafael and Eva, who developed a classic case of emotional infidelity.

CASE STUDY: EMOTIONAL INFIDELITY AT WORK

Rafael and Eva were two architects who'd been working at a large firm for more than five years. They were equally talented, and fortunate that there was no gender bias in their office. They knew each other only through small talk, as each had worked on separate projects over the years, but they were finally assigned to an important design project for a hotel. They spent at least ten hours a day together at work, sometimes more, and were under a lot of pressure. Over time their benign chitchat and work discussions became more personal, and they became better friends. When Eva looked upset on a Monday morning, Rafael would ask what was wrong, and she'd tell him that it had been a stressful weekend, with one child playing soccer and the other having a dance recital, and she and her husband, Henry, arguing about household chores. They'd been married for more than twelve years and loved each other. Henry was a good guy, though his listening skills could have been better—but he was stressed, too, with the demands of his office. Eva and Henry still worked well as a team, but their intimacy had faded.

Over time, Rafael and Eva would always spend Monday mornings talking about their weekends and their partners. Slowly the conversations became more detailed and intimate, until it got to the point where they were getting more emotional support from each other than from their partners. They hadn't planned this. Neither had ill intent. Neither wanted to have a sexual affair. The emotional infidelity wouldn't have happened if they hadn't been assigned to the same project and had to spend every day together. What became a deep connection simply snuck up on them after six months.

The exposure of their relationship began when Eva's sister was in an accident. Once she found out things would be okay, Eva talked about it all day at work with Rafael. She didn't text or call her husband. When she got home that night, she didn't tell Henry anything because she was exhausted, and her sister was going to be okay. But the next day Henry found out from another relative, and he was hurt and bewildered that Eva hadn't told him what had happened. "I thought about it," she said, "but I was really busy at work and so I told Rafael and then I forgot." Henry didn't buy it. They started fighting about other issues in their marriage that they'd been ignoring, and Henry realized that Eva had been talking to him less and less, and he felt shut out of her life. Her emotional infidelity exposed the vulnerabilities in their marriage, and they needed to decide whether to stay together or not.

In addition to being painful, emotional infidelity can be a trigger leading to the end of a relationship. This is what happened to Eva and Henry. After counseling, they decided to divorce. Eva's close relationship with Rafael was one of the primary reasons, and it helped both Eva and Henry understand that they'd irrevocably drifted apart, and that she was no longer passionately connected to her husband for a lifetime commitment. She realized she'd stopped being so close to Henry because she no longer wanted to be.

THE INFIDELITY TRIFECTA

In the worst-case scenario, a person can suffer from the "Infidelity Trifecta." The emotional infidelity deepens, what was once a platonic friendship becomes sexual, and then the unfaithful person starts hiding their out-of-control spending. Emotional infidelity can be a slippery slope that sometimes leads to both sexual and financial infidelity.

Did the Infidelity Trifecta happen to you?   Yes ☐ No ☐

RED FLAGS FOR EMOTIONAL INFIDELITY

Believe it or not, sometimes there aren't many signs of emotional infidelity. The person engaged in it often feels like there's nothing to hide—especially if the relationship is with someone the couple already knows, so it's not unusual for their name to come up.

(It's the *frequency* of the name coming up that's the warning sign.) They've simply got a close friend to confide in, and in their mind they don't feel they have anything to hide.

These are some of the signs you might see:

- Conversations about that person used to be impersonal but are now more detailed and revealing.

- Your partner tells the other person all the things they used to talk to you about. (Often, with emotional infidelity, the partner doesn't see the emotional connection as a betrayal so they might share something like, "Well, John at my office thinks this about…." Or, "John doesn't understand where you are coming from and neither do I.")

- Your partner tells the other person about the challenges in your marriage.

- You're no longer the first person your partner talks to about events that come up, special or not.

- Your partner isn't as empathetic as usual.

- Your partner is spending more time at work, often eagerly.

- People your partner used to complain about aren't mentioned anymore.

- Your partner goes out more often after hours with people from work.

- Questions that your partner used to ask you are no longer as prevalent.

- Your partner seems less curious about what's going on in *your* life.

- Your partner is texting at all hours and on the weekends—demonstrating an unusually high comfort level with someone else.

What signs of emotional infidelity did you see?

_____

_____

_____

_____

_____

_____

_____

Did you believe these signs at first? Why not?

_____

_____

_____

_____

FRIENDSHIP VERSUS EMOTIONAL INFIDELITY

We all have friends we confide in, sometimes spilling our deepest secrets to them because we know they will remain just that—secrets. Ideally, talking to friends doesn't take away from the intimacy one should have with one's partner. Furthermore, friends normally don't become anything more than friends who are simply being there for you. They aren't romantic relationships. (Of course, if that happens, it's a different story!) Confiding in them is not emotional infidelity.

The key difference is when someone tells their work (or other) friend intimate details about their life and *stops telling these details to their partner*. There is a shift in what had once been intimate or everyday conversations with their partner. This friend gets them. Listens to them. Consoles them. Gives them advice and is always eager to talk to them. When it gets to the point where one sees this person as more empathic than their partner, emotional infidelity is entrenched.

If, on the other hand, there's a friend that you just like to talk to about certain topics a bit more than to your partner, that's not emotional infidelity. The fact that a relationship is close isn't an automatic sign. Sometimes a person can get close to someone at work or school, and then when the job or school year ends there are goodbyes, and that's the end of it. Or sometimes changes in routine or conversations about other people don't mean there's infidelity. One client's partner assumed something was going on when the client was merely worried about layoffs at work, so they worked longer hours and talked about it incessantly at home because they needed to decompress.

How do you see the difference between friendship and emotional infidelity?

_____

_____

_____

HOW DID YOU FIND OUT?

Since emotional infidelity usually happens over a period of time, it might have been going on for longer than you realized. You might have known about this relationship and thought nothing of it until it had already morphed into something deeper that became glaringly obvious.

How did you find out about the emotional infidelity?

_____

_____

_____

Was there any snooping involved? If so, what did you do? (See page page 71 for more about snooping.)

_____

_____

_____

Were you absolutely certain this was emotional infidelity on your partner's part?
Yes ☐ *No* ☐

If so, why?

_____

_____

_____

When did you confront your partner?

_____

What did they say?

_____

_____

_____

Were they defensive?   Yes ☐ No ☐

Did they deny the emotional closeness?   Yes ☐ No ☐

Did they understand what you meant by emotional infidelity, or protest that they didn't?

_____

_____

Did you feel dismissed when you brought up the subject? If so, how?

_____

_____

_____

Did you ask how long it had been going on?   Yes ☐ No ☐

If so, did you believe the answer?   Yes ☐ No ☐

Did you give an ultimatum—such as "I don't want you talking to that person ever again"? Or what did you say?

_____

_____

_____

Did you know that such an ultimatum could be an impossible ask—if, for instance the situation was taking place at a job that neither could quit?   Yes ☐ No ☐

Did you contact the other person?   Yes ☐ No ☐

If so, what happened?

_____

_____

_____

_____

WHAT HURT YOU THE MOST?

I've counseled many people who were absolutely gutted by their partner's emotional infidelity—feeling far more hurt, they told me, than if there had been sexual infidelity. Some people feel that a drunken one-night stand is less threatening than a long-term emotional connection. Emotional infidelity is all inward. It's about feelings, not touching. It's about never fully knowing what was said about you, and likely never knowing the all of it.

The hardest is what Emilie said to me: "What did she give him emotionally that he couldn't get from me? He trusted her with his feelings instead of me. It made me feel totally worthless."

People who were confident in their relationship can be totally blindsided by their partner's emotional infidelity, being shaken to their very core. How, they wonder, could they have been so wrong?

What was the worst feeling you had when you found out about your partner's emotional infidelity?

_____

_____

_____

Did you feel left out? Replaced?   Yes ☐ No ☐

Did you ask your partner for specifics about what had been shared or confided with the other person?   Yes ☐ No ☐

If you got an answer, did you believe it? If not, why?

_____

_____

_____

Did you feel relieved or anything else when your suspicions were confirmed?
Yes ☐ No ☐

NEGATIVE SELF-TALK	POSITIVE REFRAMING
If I had paid more attention…	I am not at fault for this.
He was talking about me all day long.	There's no reason to think he was talking about me all day long.
Why was that person more trustworthy than me?	I won't spend time comparing myself to someone else.

CASE STUDY: WHEN A SECOND CHANCE GOES WRONG

Francisco had had a long career working as a manager in a successful downtown hotel that had a nightclub. That's where he met Maxime, who worked there as well. They got married when they were in their early twenties. She knew the temptations of hotel and club life, with attractive out-of-towners with lowered inhibitions hitting on her husband, but she trusted him. Fifteen years later, however, Maxime caught him sexting someone who'd also been working in the club for many years, though there was no sexual affair. There was a lot of anger on her part and guilt on his, but they worked through it. Then, a year later, she caught him sexting the same woman again. At this point she didn't feel like she could trust him ever again, and the relationship ended.

When she came to see me, she was angry and sad. She thought they had worked on their relationship and felt they had turned a corner. This felt like a double betrayal to her. Now she doubted everything he said.

Does this story resonate with you? How so?

_____

_____

_____

CHAPTER 6
FINANCIAL INFIDELITY

"There is nothing more humiliating than loving someone
so much that you forgive the infidelities."

—Jerry Hall

"What am I going to do?"

That's usually the visceral response people have when realizing they are the victims of financial infidelity. That happens when (as you read in Chapter 1) your partner hasn't told you the truth about their spending—when there is any hiding, dissembling, or secrets about finances.

We all know that people cheat, but we don't often imagine that the cheating will involve our trusted partner spending down or stealing our money. Doubtless you've had a friend or acquaintance who has had a gambling or addiction problem, but you probably didn't think this friend was surreptitiously siphoning off the savings to pay for his addictions or to take care of his family but for his girlfriends.

Money is always a loaded issue. Being in debt keeps many unhappy couples from breaking up—and debts make everything worse when bills can't get paid. It is harder to break up when in debt, and some people try to work it out. Every situation is different.

While sexual or emotional infidelity can break your heart, financial infidelity can break *you*, period. Talk about a brutal betrayal! There is no price tag on the hurt of finding your partner involved with another person, but there is a definite price tag when the money you need for basic survival skills—your literal safety net—is gone. That can destroy your immediate plans and your hopes for the future.

This might be especially true if you're one of the millions of Americans living paycheck to paycheck. The numbers are dismal for how much people are able to save. Retiring at sixty-five, as our parents or grandparents once easily did, has pretty much become a myth. And no matter how wealthy you are, you're worth less single than together. The higher earner might take a hit during a divorce but can then recoup their losses as time goes on, but the lower earner might take years and years, if ever, to regain their lost financial status. Credit card debt can haunt you for years to come.

THE RED FLAGS OF FINANCIAL INFIDELITY

There are so many ways to discover financial infidelity—especially if banking and bill-paying are done online, where it's easy to check statements. And it can be hard to remember what was done with an account set up years ago. Many discoveries of financial infidelity are accidental; some red flags are listed in Chapter 1, but here are a few more.

- You see changes to basic financial patterns or budget. You notice that a few hundred dollars have been withdrawn here and there, yet nothing new was purchased.

- You notice changes to your partner's behavior patterns.

- Your credit score has changed for seemingly no reason.

- Your partner suddenly wants to economize.

- Your partner wants to defer a large purchase or life event that you'd been planning, such as buying a house or having a baby, because they're having an affair and aren't sure they want to stay in the relationship.

- You're locked out of your partner's phone, tablet, or computer, even though you wouldn't dream of snooping.

- You get notices in the mail about unpaid bills.

- You see payments for restaurants or hotels in the next town, and you know you've never been there and there's no reason for your partner to have stayed there.

- You get a notification in the mail to verify changes or an added bank account, credit card, or password.

- You get an alert for potential fraud for a large purchase—one you didn't make.

- A package was sent to another address from your Amazon account.

- You notice unusual purchases. One client discovered financial infidelity when his wife bought a vanity plate for her secret boyfriend's new car!

- You share email accounts. (This is almost always done by seniors, but it's not something I recommend for anyone at any age, as you do need your privacy!)

FINANCIAL REPERCUSSIONS

There are two aspects to financial infidelity—financial repercussions and emotional repercussions.

How did you discover the financial infidelity?

_____

_____

_____

How did you confront your partner about it?

_____

_____

What was the response?

_____

_____

What was your response?

_____

_____

How much did the financial infidelity impact your day-to-day living expenses?

_____

_____

_____

How much did it impact your short-term living expenses?

_____

_____

_____

How much did it impact your long-term expenses?

_____

_____

_____

Will you be able to recoup any losses fairly quickly?   Yes ☐ No ☐

What purchase or life event have you had to put off because of financial infidelity?

_____

What is most different about how you're living now?

_____

_____

_____

JOINT FINANCES AND PAPERWORK

Dealing with joint finances after a relationship ends due to financial infidelity can be difficult, since you will have to communicate in some way with your ex. But figuring out who owns what or who deals with what paperwork is just as painful. Often you're not going to think about certain things until you get the bills.

Round 1 is dealing with what the two of you had together in your home. Who gets what? Who assesses the value? Was that bicycle a gift to you or to your partner? Who gets the security deposit refund if you both move out? Round 2 may involve the storage unit, if you have one. Who pays the monthly charges? Who divvies up what's inside?

As for legal paperwork, you might have made your sister-in-law the custodian for your children in your will. You never dreamed that you'd be dealing with the end of your relationship and that you no longer want that kind of tie to your ex's family.

All these situations need to be dealt with, sooner rather than later—which is not easy when you're worried about your overhead and might need to move or take on a second job just to make ends meet. Be sure to get legal advice about joint accounts and speak to your bank and credit card companies as well. Make sure you have all the passwords you need, and print out hard copies of everything for your records.

If you had joint accounts, list them here—banking, credit cards, etc.

_____   _____

_____   _____

_____   _____

_____   _____

Who was authorized to do your banking and bill-paying? Are both of you still authorized?

_____

What paperwork do you need to redo, such as your will or life insurance beneficiaries?

_____

_____

_____

FINANCIAL ASSISTANCE

If you are unexpectedly strapped for cash, are there trusted people in your orbit whom you can ask for help? For all of us, especially if we're used to being financially self-sufficient, it can be difficult to ask for help. But you may need to do so, especially if you have to pay for lawyers, which can be incredibly expensive.

Let's say you're thirty-three and your parents spent a lot of their savings on your wedding and on a down payment for your condo. Now, eight years later, they are dealing with their own worries about their financial future and can't help you as they once did; they might be able to take you in but not bail you out when you are in the prime of your money-making life. And if your credit is not stellar, it can be hard to get help from a bank or other financial institution. Living off credit cards can lead to extremely high interest rates and other woes.

CASE STUDY: WHEN MONEY COMES WITH STRINGS ATTACHED

Here's what happened to Kelly when she got divorced after her husband spent their savings on his girlfriend. She received some child support, but money was tight and she had two small children to take care of.

"I asked my wealthy father for help, but his way of controlling me was to give me less than I needed," she told me. "I was very grateful for the money, but an extra few hundred dollars was not going to spoil me, considering that he was a multimillionaire. He felt I needed to be taught a lesson—he'd help me out, but not with enough to take away the problem. When my daughter had unexpected medical expenses and I needed $2,000, he gave me $1,500. And when I went to graduate school for my MFA, he refused to loan me any money because he thought it was a terrible idea. It took me years to pay off my student loans. But he would have paid for everything if what I'd studied had been his idea, like an MBA. On top of that, my mother also had her form of control. If I liked something as a teenager and she didn't, I had to pay for it. But if she liked it, she would buy two. Just to rub it in!"

Whom could you ask for help?

_____

_____

_____

_____

Was this hard to do?   Yes ☐ No ☐

Did you get the funds you needed?   Yes ☐ No ☐

If so, were they enough?   Yes ☐ No ☐

Do you have a backup plan? If so, what is it?

_____

_____

Have you set up a schedule for repayment, if one is expected?   Yes ☐ No ☐

CASE STUDY: WHEN FINANCIAL INFIDELITY REALLY HURTS

Grace Wang was married to her husband, Jimmy, for more than thirty years—nearly as long as Jimmy had been working with her father, Charlie, as his right-hand man at their Asian toy company. (That's how the couple had met.) Their marriage had been unhappy for years, but when she discovered that Jimmy had a mistress living in an apartment he paid for, that was the last straw.

This would have been a typical scenario of fighting over finances, but it gets worse. After hiring a forensic accountant because she figured that Jimmy had been stashing some of his income offshore, she found out that her very own father had sided with her ex. Talk about unintended consequences! Her father regarded Jimmy as the son he'd never had, so when Jimmy moved out, Charlie paid for that apartment and gave him a substantial chunk of interest in the company—something he'd never done when Jimmy and Grace had been married. Charlie completely disregarded all the work Grace had done for the company over the years, such as coming up with ideas for toys and working in the office when needed.

Grace was totally devastated and found it impossible to reconcile with her father after he'd hurt her so badly. The final blow came when Charlie died, and in his will he left his business to Jimmy. At that point Grace needed the money far more than Jimmy did. For her to overcome her grief and bitterness was difficult, and it took her years to not be justifiably bitter at the betrayal. Knowing that your father and your ex-husband were in cahoots is a devastatingly cruel blow.

UNINTENDED CIRCUMSTANCES

As I've mentioned already, the shock of financial infidelity and the need to deal with the immediate fallout can be devastating. You need good legal and financial advice about any debt accumulated during the marriage, and how much is shared or not. If both your names are on a mortgage title, for example, you are both liable for payments.

For many couples, one person is primarily involved in paying bills and overseeing expenditures. If that was you, great! You're already on top of everything. If not, the fact that your now-ex had the power over financial decisions has doubtless created an enormous problem.

One of the most common unintended circumstances after financial infidelity is needing to learn to manage the bills and the budget. I always encourage couples to both be very aware and on top of all their finances so they can take care of everything at a moment's notice—to know when, where, and how the bills arrive and how they should be paid. If your partner had had an accident, would you have been able to take over? Was the life insurance premium due? And if you didn't pay it on time, would it be cancelled? Should you tap into your 401K? Or any college funds? (The answer should be to do so only as a last resort.) Do you have to pull your children out of private school and disrupt their school year?

Another enormous issue is when you have to get a job, change jobs, or take on an additional job. Reinventing yourself is hard for anyone, but those who've been stay-at-home parents for any amount of time will not only have to explain the gap in their resumes, but the workplace is likely to have changed since they were last employed.

What unintended financial circumstances happened to you? List as many as you need to.

_____   _____

_____   _____

_____   _____

_____   _____

How did you manage them?

_____

_____

_____

_____

_____

Are they now resolved?　　Yes ☐　No ☐

BE PROACTIVE

There's being proactive about a painful situation because you *want* to be and being proactive because you *have* to be. Feeling powerless about your current financial situation can lead to a shutdown at a time when that can cause even more financial harm in the future.

What's very helpful is to take at least one action to tackle your money issues right now. (Stalking your ex on social media to see what they're spending is not one of them!) It's time to get your money mojo back when the worst shock has worn off, as this is a situation that can't be put off. Set small goals that will be easy to attain. For example, write a spreadsheet, make an appointment to see your bank manager and accountant, or call your credit card companies. Ask friends and loved ones for advice, if you can. Don't go it alone.

Taking action will help with any feelings of powerlessness. There are many professionals, and hopefully family members, who can steer you in the right direction when you are feeling financially overwhelmed. You might be surprised at how many people have had financial woes they never talked about because the situation was just too private or painful.

What can you do today to make yourself feel less helpless and out of control?

_____

_____

_____

_____

Once things settle down, do you feel empowered by now having to take care of all your finances on your own? Yes ☐ No ☐

What has been the hardest thing to do?

_____

_____

How did you do it?

_____

_____

_____

EMOTIONAL REPERCUSSIONS

Your partner might have done something like this when you were sitting together in bed, after you'd just kissed good night—with only a few swipes on their phone, signed up for a dating site or set up a new bank account. The thing about money is that it's not just for goods and purchases; you can take away someone's control with just one swipe.

The emotional impact of financial infidelity cannot be understated. Not only does it make it hard for you to trust *anyone* about any money issues again, but it can trigger a deep and justified rage at the betrayal that hurt you deeply and upended your life. This is often compounded by your being mad not just at your ex but at yourself for missing or diminishing any red flags. But now is not the time to beat yourself up!

How did your anger manifest itself? Toward your partner and/or yourself?

_____

_____

_____

_____

_____

Over time, has your anger or its frequency changed?   Yes ☐ No ☐

If so, how has it changed?

_____

_____

Has it gotten in the way of your work life?   Yes ☐ No ☐

If so, how?

_____

_____

_____

Are you shutting down from other people?   Yes ☐ No ☐

Who in your life have you told about this situation?

_____

_____

_____

_____

How did it feel to tell them?

_____

_____

_____

Were they helpful or not?   Yes ☐ No ☐

Are you depressed or anxious about money matters?   Yes ☐ No ☐

How did you explain the circumstances to the children? (See page 123 for more on this topic.)

_____

_____

_____

THE **COURAGE** TO **WALK AWAY**

Some people who've suffered through financial infidelity blame themselves. I hope that's not you! Let's put shame where it belongs: on the person who upended your financial security.

Still, there can be shame when having to deal with what to say to people you know. Close friends and family members should be supportive, of course, but it's everyone else in your orbit that can leave you at a loss. If, for instance, you used to donate generously to school functions, you might need to save up for the kids' needs now, so you have to stretch your spending differently. Yet at the same time, you have every right *not* to have to discuss your private life and/or changed circumstances and social status unless you really want to. This can be tricky to navigate.

Did you feel any shame about your changed circumstances? If so, why?

_____

_____

_____

Do you still feel any shame? Are there certain triggers?

_____

_____

_____

What do you tell yourself to make yourself feel better about a challenging situation?

_____

_____

_____

Instead of going over every "what-if" and "why-didn't-I," reframe these negatives with positive statements instead, such as shown on the next page.

NEGATIVE SELF-TALK	POSITIVE REFRAMING
Why did I trust him with our money?	I had no reason not to trust.
What made me ignore the red flags?	I will be more proactive in the future.
Why didn't I check the bills every month?	I will stay on top of my expenses now.
I was so stupid….	I wasn't stupid; I was trusting.
Why didn't I….	I will stop blaming myself and learn from this.

REBUILDING FINANCIAL TRUST

Sure, you don't expect to trust a car salesperson. And after financial infidelity, how can you ever trust anyone about money? You don't want to be burned again, so you're likely looking for ways to protect yourself emotionally from future harm.

How to do this? Believe, but *verify*. Be upfront with a future partner about what happened, as it will show up in little ways in how you spend money in the future. Your future partner should be understanding and sympathetic—but be careful not to make accusations, because this new person in your life is *not* your ex!

It's not always the dollar amount. It's more about having a system in place and knowing your safety net is secure to give you peace of mind for the future. Sometimes wealthy people cut coupons or save for sales because they come from a place of fear. For some, it's knowing they have X amount in savings; for others, it's being able to cover the monthly overhead on time.

The good news is that once you've gotten your money management back in order, you will know how to manage your finances responsibly. Hopefully you'll have many successful strategies about earning power in the future.

What would make you feel financially stable and secure again?

_____

_____

_____

_____

How different do you want your money management to be from now on?

_____

_____

_____

_____

What does being financially comfortable look like to you?

_____

_____

_____

_____

We change our behavior based on past experiences, so what would you do differently in the future?

_____

_____

_____

_____

CHAPTER 7

HEALING FROM THE FALLOUT WITH FRIENDS, FAMILY, AND CHILDREN

"Love is understood, in a historical way, as one of the great human vocations—but its counterspell has always been infidelity. This terrible, terrible betrayal that can tear apart not only another person, not only oneself, but whole families."

—Junot Diaz

Part of working through infidelity includes dealing with the important loved ones in your inner circle and their response to it. Because the changes in your life will likely affect your parents, other family members, and close friends, they may want to jump in, for good or bad, and whether you want them to or not.

Ideally, you want support on your terms, but that might not happen. They might feel they have the right to tell you how to behave, or what changes to make. They might minimize the situation. They might even tell you to give your ex another chance, saying things like, "But they've been so good in so many other ways!" even after you've made it clear that it's not an option.

Of course, people who care about you will want to help, but it's very important for you to be mindful that any advice or comments they give you are based on what *they* would do in your situation.

DEALING WITH YOUR FRIENDS

Your friends are not your therapist—even if they want to be. Every infidelity situation is different, just as every relationship is different. Even if your friends have gone through their own painful breakup with their own ex after infidelity, their advice will be based on what worked for them and their own framework and personalities at the time. What they tell you could be helpful or might not be useful at all.

Some of my clients have several trusted friends who have helped them navigate the infidelity waters with compassion and patience. Others had only one friend to rely on, but for them, that one was more than enough. They were profoundly grateful to have had such emotional support when they needed it most.

Still others were very let down when they realized friends they thought they could trust and meant well were not helpful, or were gossiping about their situation. I hope this didn't happen to you!

IDENTIFY YOUR SUPPORT SYSTEM NOW

Which friends can you count on? List them here.

_____

_____

_____

_____

_____

_____

Why can you count on them?

_____

_____

_____

_____

_____

_____

Have you been able to discuss unpleasant details with someone?   Yes ☐ No ☐

Did anyone step up unexpectedly? In what way?

_____

_____

_____

_____

What did you say to tell that person how much their help means to you?

_____

_____

UNWANTED ADVICE FROM FRIENDS

Help isn't helpful unless it's asked for!

Just because somebody means well doesn't make their advice the best option for you. Many of us have friends who automatically try to fix things, but this is not a situation for them to fix. As mentioned earlier in this chapter, their advice is predicated on their own history when presented with similar circumstances. I've had plenty of clients tell me that friends actually got angry when their advice was ignored, and this is painful for everyone.

When you're vulnerable and hurt, judging whether to act on any kind of advice can be difficult. You're coming from a traumatic place, so don't try to make major decisions until things have calmed down and you're feeling stronger.

Was there any advice that absolutely floored you (good or bad)?

_____

_____

_____

_____

Did anyone tell you to get back together with your ex?   Yes ☐ No ☐

If so, what was their reasoning?

_____

_____

_____

Do you wonder if they are fearful that being single is hard?   Yes ☐ No ☐

WHEN YOUR FRIENDS KNEW BEFORE YOU DID

If your friends knew about the infidelity before you did, this is one of those tricky situations where they're damned if they tell you and damned if they don't. Even if you would want to know, that doesn't mean that somebody else would. There's usually no right answer.

Often your friends just don't know what to do, especially if they had suspicions about your ex's infidelity but no hard proof. It was either hearsay or innuendo, and they didn't want to make accusations if they weren't sure they were 100 percent accurate. Or they might not have wanted to believe the evidence, so they thought silence was best. These friends want to be there for you and to be totally honest, but this may be new territory for them; they want to tell you but don't want to hurt you—or be blamed for a breakup. If they do tell you, it can cause your anger or frustration to be projected onto them.

Not being told, on the other hand, can put a wedge in your friendship, as you might be angry and upset that they were hiding the truth from you. You might think it would help to have a hypothetical conversation, such as "If you had a family history of a genetic disease, would you want to know?" Or "If your partner was cheating, would you want to know?" But if someone suspects a friend's partner is unfaithful, these questions are too obvious. Most people would say, "Why are you asking me that?"—opening the door to a room you may not want to enter. Here's the tricky part—you could say you'd want to know (or wouldn't want to know), but until you're in a *real* and not hypothetical situation, you can't predict how you'll respond. (It's sort of like couples who are happy to tell everyone how they'll behave as parents and then doing the opposite of everything they were so sure of once the kids arrive with minds of their own!)

Sometimes a friend will discover the infidelity and confront the unfaithful person first. If so, an ultimatum such as "If you don't tell your partner, I will" can be enough to elicit a confession. Or perhaps not. If the unfaithful person is given the opportunity to come clean, that takes the onus off the friend. But if the infidelity continues, the same situation of not knowing what to do rears its tricky head for the friend.

If something was going on, would you want to know?   Yes ☐ No ☐

Did you ask your friends what they saw, or what your relationship seemed to be from their point of view?   Yes ☐ No ☐

If they knew about the infidelity, were they the ones to tell you?   Yes ☐ No ☐

If they did know but didn't tell you, how does that make you feel?

_____

_____

_____

_____

Did you confront them about this?   Yes ☐ No ☐

If so, what did you say?

_____

_____

_____

Are you worried about trust issues? For example, do you think they might know something else that they don't want to tell you?   Yes ☐ No ☐

If so, did you ask them for details? What did they say?

_____

_____

Are you afraid they might gossip?   Yes ☐ No ☐

GIVING AND GETTING MIXED SIGNALS

When you're in turmoil, it can be hard to find a happy medium with your friends. Some people shut down and withdraw, but I've found that people are more likely to be in need of talking. If you were used to talking to your ex about nearly everything, you might feel an intense need to have your friends be temporary surrogates filling the void for that kind of emotional intimacy.

You can lose objectivity and not be aware of how needy you are. For example, you're on the phone with or texting a friend for a long time and they may be trying to end the conversation, but you're unaware of their hints. If you've spent two hours venting (justifiably) about your ex, and only then ask what's going on in their lives, eventually they might not want to be so responsive.

Be aware of how you're treating your friends. You certainly don't want to wear them out but might be doing so unwittingly. Dealing with infidelity and the upheaval in your life can be a long process, so it's understandable if this is all you want to talk about initially. But if it continues to be *all* you want to talk about, your friends can balk.

Check in with your friends. Ask them if you're overwhelming them, and say that you want them to let you know how much sharing is best for them. For example, you might tell them something like, "I need to know what's not okay. I don't want you to answer the phone just because I called. Please tell me if it's not a good time."

That's what my client Tracey, a nurse, finally was able to do. "My best friend, Deirdre, went through a really bad breakup after her husband was unfaithful," she told me. "After nearly eight months of her calling me to talk late at night, I had to be blunt. I told her I always wanted to be there for her, but I worked all day at a very stressful job, and nighttime was when I needed to decompress for my own health and sanity. Then I told her to not call me after 7 p.m. She got a bit huffy at first, but then she realized how demanding she'd been, and we worked out a schedule when I'd be available for her without watching the clock, and vice versa. She had to be reminded that I had my own stuff to deal with, too."

Do you think that you are having too many conversations about the infidelity?
Yes ☐ *No* ☐

Are your friends avoiding you lately? In what manner?

_____

_____

_____

If so, what reasons are you hearing?

_____

_____

_____

_____

SOCIAL ISOLATION

Not wanting to deal with other people when you're feeling vulnerable and blue is completely understandable. Sometimes you just don't have the energy to talk, even if you have loving friends who are there for you. But if you notice over time that your isolation has become chronic and you're still feeling shut down, be aware that too much of anything is never a good thing. If you feel just as intensely about your ex and what happened several months later, you might want to consider talking to a therapist. Sometimes people realize they can't manage emotional turmoil by themselves. If a friend says to you, "Well, you know, when I had a really difficult situation a while ago, I went to a therapist and it really helped," take their comment as well intentioned and figure out what you can do to feel better.

Are you still isolating yourself, several months after your relationship ended, in ways you didn't initially?   Yes ☐ No ☐

Are you turning down invites?   Yes ☐ No ☐

What are your reasons?

_____

_____

How do your friends react?

_____

_____

_____

Have you made future plans?   Yes ☐ No ☐

Are you isolating yourself because you're exhausted, busy, depressed, or anything else?
Yes ☐ No ☐

CASE STUDY: WHEN YOUR FRIENDS ARE THERE FOR YOU

Marina had trouble with trust because of how she had been raised. "My mother told me I had a great childhood, but that was a big fat lie," she told me. "But she wanted me to think that, so I believed it for a long time—until I didn't." Marina didn't grow up with any feelings of safety, because she was constantly belittled and made to feel that she had no value as a person or a member of her family.

When her husband was unfaithful, Marina shut down. But her best friend stepped up in this time of need. She was the type of person who asked very pointed questions about what she could do to help, and she also knew when to step back. Shy didn't pry or give advice.

The best kind of friend is one who doesn't tell you what to do. Sometimes you have to tell your friends that you don't need their road map. Instead, all you want is for them to hear you out so that you can process what has happened. Being a good listener is the greatest gift we can give our loved ones, especially in times of distress.

WHO GETS THE MUTUAL FRIENDS?

Losing a close friend can be just as painful as losing an ex. This happens often when couples who are friends with other couples split up. It's one thing if the friends were people only you knew before you and your ex became a couple—you've got the rights, as it were, to claim them. If mutual friends feel that they have to pick sides, though—and they pick your ex—this can feel like a double or triple loss. When your ex is gone, you might feel like you've lost your sense of identity with other couples as well. It can be awkward if you and your ex were good friends with a certain couple, particularly you and the wife, and now she feels she has to pretend they aren't socializing with your ex and his new girlfriend. The hurt can be compounded.

"What upset me the most," said my client Toni, "was when my friend Ellie called and said, 'I'm here for you. Mark and I are both here for you. Don't let what happened get in the way of the things we liked to do together.' And then she ghosted me. I figured that she didn't know how to handle things, so she did nothing. But it still made me feel awful. They weren't just my ex's friends—they were a big part of my life. We'd spent so much time together over the years, and I didn't have any other friends like her. I still miss her."

If you don't want your friends to talk to or interact with your ex, tell them so. If you aren't specific about what you'd prefer at this moment, how will they know? If you find out that your friends are still in touch with your ex, you can discuss this with them, so they understand why it is difficult for you.

CASE STUDY: WHEN FRIENDS LET YOU DOWN

"I had a bad breakup with Jody after she had an affair," Luisa told me. "And then she contacted two of my close friends and tried to be friends with them. That made me very uncomfortable. One friend, Samantha, jumped on it, and that pissed me off to no end. Her attitude was, Well, tough, why should I lose Jody as a friend just because we broke up? I guess some people do feel that way. My feeling toward Samantha changed. She lost me and got my ex instead. Over time we sort of patched things up, which made life easier as we still have a lot of mutual friends, but I won't ever be able to trust Samantha or be as close to her as I was once was."

For some, on the other hand, it's a relief when certain friends are no longer around, especially if your ex really liked being with them and you didn't. You'll no longer need to make any awkward excuses to avoid them!

THE **COURAGE** TO **WALK AWAY**

How did you and your ex deal with mutual friends?

_____

_____

_____

_____

What did you do if you and your ex were claiming the same friends?

_____

_____

_____

_____

How did this make you feel?

_____

_____

_____

_____

Were you ghosted by any mutual friends you thought would always be there for you?
Yes ☐ No ☐

THE THREAT OF BEING SINGLE

A common, discouraging, and often ridiculous response to a newly single person is that they are now perceived as a threat to couples. This, of course, says far more about couples' fears about the strength of *their* relationships than it does about your behavior, but it can still sting when you are suddenly shunned by people you've known, liked, and trusted for years. This especially hurts if you realize that they only saw you as half of a unit, not as your own person—or if you become the pariah in your former social circle or at school (if you have kids) when you're not the person who was unfaithful!

CASE STUDY: WHY IS BEING SINGLE PERCEIVED AS A THREAT?

"One of the few things that made me roll my eyes and laugh after my divorce was the reaction of my neighbor, Anna," I was told by Mary Catherine. "Her husband is a deadbeat who drinks too much, hasn't seen a gym in years, has questionable hygiene, is the opposite of me politically, and yells at their dog. In other words, he's the last man I'd ever, *ever* dream of wanting to be with. Yet Anna was convinced I had designs on him. I was so glad she thought that, as it cut down on the time I had to deal with either of them!"

Another client, Kelly, told me about her neighbor Alison. They lived on the tenth floor of a large apartment building in Brooklyn. Their kids were the same age, and Alison was really helpful after Kelly's divorce (caused by her husband's infidelity), arranging playdates after school. Alison's husband, Jackson, was a tech guy, and Kelly hired him to help with the family computers. Every time Jackson came to Kelly's apartment to work—usually for no more than twenty minutes at a time—Alison would show up a few minutes later with some excuse. It took Kelly a while to realize why she did that. It had never occurred to her that Alison would think of her as a threat to her husband. The recent divorce had changed Allison's perception of her friend, and Kelly found it pathetic, more than anything else, that Allison could be so insecure and suspicious. "Believe me," Kelly told me, "Even thinking about another man was the last thing on my mind at that time! And she knew that, but it didn't make a dent in her paranoia!"

What signs did you see that people you knew were giving you odd signals about their partners?

_____

_____

_____

_____

_____

Did you say or do anything in response? If so, what?

_____

_____

_____

How did this make you feel?

_____

_____

_____

_____

UNINTENDED CIRCUMSTANCES, GOOD AND BAD

Go through the following checklist and mark any unintended circumstances that you experienced. Add your own unique experiences to the list.

- ☐ You no longer have to hang out with his best friend or any of his friends that you don't like.
- ☐ You don't have to go on vacation with those friends, either.
- ☐ You have more time to see the friends you enjoy.
- ☐ You learned who was there for you.
- ☐ You have gratitude for people who showed up in ways you needed.
- ☐ You're more aware of what you need in a friend.
- ☐ You learned how to navigate difficult situations.
- ☐ You can create your own future.

_____

_____

_____

DEALING WITH YOUR FAMILY

All family units have patterns, and these patterns tend to lead to predicable behavior. Are your parents and/or siblings mediator types? Volatile and quick to anger? Instantly judgmental? Forgiving to a fault?

Even if your family's reactions to tough situations are something you can pretty much predict—perhaps someone else had to deal with infidelity, and you were there to see and hear it all—you won't know how they will respond to *you* until it happens. The only thing you can know is that they can either make things better for you (by offering unconditional love and support on your terms) or worse (by blaming you, telling you not to split up, or creating more conflict by triggering fights about you and your ex).

What you want to hear is "I am so sorry. What can we do to help?" What you might hear instead is "Listen to me, because I'm the only one who knows what you have to do now about that low-life." Or perhaps "I am your mother, and I know what is best for you." Some families see trouble in a marriage as an opportunity to put their stamp on what happens next, and if so you will be caught in the middle. They might do things without your permission, such as contacting your ex or talking badly about them to your children or friends. In the worst-case scenario, they will blame you for your partner's infidelity, and that would be incredibly painful. Knowing that some people feel compelled to blame someone, no matter what the situation is, doesn't take the sting away. That's not what you're looking for in terms of support!

TELLING YOUR FAMILY WHAT HAPPENED

Telling family members about the infidelity you experienced is not an easy task. Your expectations of what might or might not happen can have your imagination running wild. There's no one right or wrong way to do this, except that you want to avoid being defensive. But be prepared to say as much as you can without skirting the issue. For instance, saying something like, "We grew apart" if you don't want to tell the whole story will instantly raise suspicions. Your family will likely be perceptive enough to realize you're only discussing the appetizer—What will you say when the main course arrives?

But do pick a calm time when there's no other noticeable stress to contend with, such as work or health issues. Say only what you want to; *you* control the narrative. Your family might want answers you're not ready to give. Simply tell them that. You are under no obligation to go into details. But be aware that this is where guilt-tripping can come in, especially if you don't feel comfortable sharing unpleasant details about infidelity.

What has been the hardest thing for you to tell your family? What made that so hard?

_____

_____

_____

_____

How much of the truth did you feel comfortable sharing?

_____

Did you hide any of the truth from your family? What, specifically?

_____

_____

_____

If so, why?

_____

_____

What were you expecting to happen?

_____

_____

_____

Were you fearful of a strong response?

_____

_____

_____

Or that you would have to deal with your family's disappointment?   Yes ☐ No ☐

Were you afraid that talking about the infidelity would hurt them? (Many people feel this way, especially if their family has had a close and loving relationship with the ex.)
Yes ☐ No ☐

Were you ashamed or embarrassed, or both?

_____

_____

_____

Is there anything you wanted to say to your family but haven't said yet?

_____

_____

_____

Were you surprised by anyone disappearing or being unkind?   Yes ☐ No ☐

What did that person say or do?

_____

_____

_____

Are you able to limit contact with family members who haven't been helpful?
Yes ☐ No ☐

UNWANTED OR UNHELPFUL ADVICE

Just because somebody means well doesn't mean that what they suggest will be the best choice for you. Family members can sometimes feel they have the right to tell you what to do. If they become pushy or intrusive, it might help to mitigate the buttinskies by saying something like "Thank you for your concern. I appreciate it and will take it into consideration"—and then ignoring it. It's best to avoid saying "Thank you for your advice" if you don't want advice!

Did you get unwanted or unhelpful advice?   Yes ☐ No ☐

If so, what unwanted advice did you get?

_____

_____

_____

_____

_____

What unhelpful advice did you get?

_____

_____

_____

_____

Were you surprised by any comments?   Yes ☐ No ☐

If so, how did you respond?

_____

_____

_____

_____

WHAT TO SAY WHEN YOU DON'T WANT TO TALK ABOUT IT

- I appreciate your concern, but I'm just not ready to talk about this.

- I need to process this on my own before I start sharing the details.

- It's too painful to talk about right now.

- Right now, I just need to know that you are here for me.

- Can I call you when I'm ready to talk?

ESTABLISHING PRIVACY BOUNDARIES

Infidelity is a painful and private topic, and it is nobody's business but yours. As I've said, _you_ are the one who controls the narrative. You might feel comfortable sharing some details with a sibling or cousin you trust rather than your parents, for example, or you might not. You don't want to hide your partner's harmful behavior at your own expense, though. (This can be an issue if there are children and the grandparents are wondering if this will affect visitations, for instance.) How much to talk about will be based on your gut feeling at the time—and you won't know that until the time comes.

What were you able to say to establish boundaries?

_____

_____

_____

_____

Have family members kept pushing for more information? In what way?

_____

_____

_____

_____

If so, how have you managed this?

_____

_____

_____

_____

IDENTIFY YOUR SUPPORT SYSTEM NOW

Family members can be there for you—or not.

Which family members can you count on? List them here.

_____

_____

_____

_____

_____

_____

Why can you count on them?

_____

_____

_____

_____

_____

_____

Have you been able to discuss unpleasant details with them? Yes ☐ No ☐

Has anyone stepped up unexpectedly? In what way?

_____

_____

_____

_____

What did you say to let that person know how much their help means to you?

_____

_____

_____

DEALING WITH CHILDREN

Child educator John Holt once said, "If I had to make a general rule for living and working with children, it might be this: be wary of saying or doing anything to a child that you would not do to another adult, whose good opinion and affection you valued."

If you and your ex had children together, this adds another layer of difficulty to your healing, as a constant reminder of what you have lost. If your children are too young to understand what happened and you can't tell them the truth, that makes it even harder. Your life situation has changed so much; you are hurting, and the kids are also hurting. When you are in pain, and especially when you are angry, it can be difficult to bite your tongue about what your ex did—but you always need to be there for your children, the way you need your friends to be there for you.

Unless your ex moves far away and has little contact with your children, you will have to navigate the awkwardness of seeing your ex and his family members at holiday or family events, school functions, or pickups/dropoffs for the foreseeable future. Your children's needs are paramount. Ask yourself what decisions complement your narrative of what is best for the children. Answering that question will lead you to make better decisions.

TELLING YOUR CHILDREN WHAT HAPPENED

Having age-appropriate explanations and conversations with your children will be a challenge, no matter how old or mature they are. There's no one specific strategy, as your conversations will be tailored to their age, their personalities, and their relationship with your ex. If, for example, your child is in the hero-worshipping stage with your ex, anger and upset with *you* might be ongoing for a while. Or if your child already had a rocky relationship with your ex and had a pretty good idea that there were serious issues, there might be pain and confusion but also relief.

Before you say anything to your children, ask yourself what you can say that's in their best interests and that won't make them hate your ex. Keep the worst details private. Sometimes saying too much creates more questions than answers. Be as calm as possible. It's okay to be sad, because you *are* sad. Your children will eventually figure things out when they're old enough to process the truth.

Never say anything to them about the situation or about your ex from a place of anger. Even if your ex's behavior was egregious, you don't want to trash your ex—or any of your ex's family members—to your children. This can be hard, especially if those family members are pushing your buttons. But your children are not responsible for any of these conflicts, and they should be shielded from them. Their best interests right now are more important than your need to be right or to be the injured party.

How did you tell the kids in an age-appropriate way?

_____

_____

_____

_____

_____

What was their reaction?

_____

_____

_____

_____

Did any aspect of that reaction surprise you? If so, what was surprising?

_____

_____

_____

How did you respond, whatever their reaction was?

_____

_____

_____

How have you continued the conversations over time?

_____

_____

_____

_____

CO-PARENTING THE CHILDREN

Working out the details of co-parenting can be painful, especially when you are still hurting from the infidelity. Be mindful of wanting to hurt your ex back, because this would also hurt the children—who are too often used as pawns in this situation. The bottom line should always be for you to go back to what best serves your children's needs. Most likely that will mean seeing your ex as much as is feasible, even if that is hard for you to accept right now.

What are the terms of your child custody arrangements?

_____

_____

_____

_____

_____

_____

_____

_____

_____

_____

Is this what you wanted? Why or why not?

_____

_____

_____

_____

If not, are there still ongoing legal issues?   *Yes* ☐ *No* ☐

How has your ex behaved around the children?

_____

_____

_____

_____

What will you do if your decisions regarding the children are upended by your ex?

_____

_____

_____

_____

If there are ongoing problems with co-parenting, what steps can you take to mitigate them?

_____

_____

_____

_____

CHAPTER 8
STRATEGIES FOR STRESS RELIEF

"You don't have to see the whole staircase, just take the first step."

—Martin Luther King

After a relationship ends, the stress likely won't be going anywhere anytime soon. But now, more than ever, you need to be taking care of your health. This needs to be an absolute priority, even if your schedule is fraught, because stress can damage every aspect of your ability to function, both physically and emotionally. This is an unavoidable biological fact.

I ask my clients who are dealing with infidelity to challenge themselves. They're working from their fear, which is a feeling. People often describe how they feel as if it is a *fact* and not merely a feeling in that moment. When you make any thought a fact, it shapes everything that comes after, including how you deal with stress.

For example, someone who has been deeply hurt might find themselves still making excuses for their partner, saying "It wasn't so bad" or "Maybe it was my fault," while trying to talk themselves back into the relationship. Or perhaps they hear the echo of their mother saying, "It's so hard to find a partner, you know what I mean…." An understandable part of their fear is that they don't want to be alone. And they don't want to deal with thinking that everyone in their orbit knows intimate details about the infidelity. For them, the known is better than the unknown.

With all the choices that come with the aftermath of infidelity—whether you're making them because you're scared or because it's the right thing for you to do—it's the not yet knowing about the future that is so stress-inducing. That can cause anxiety and worries.

Often when we are in the throes of profound stress due to a trauma such as infidelity, the situation kidnaps logic. It kidnaps typical responses. It amplifies everything. When you make decisions based on fear you don't usually make the best choices, because fear clouds judgment.

Ask yourself: "Is this true, or is this my fear speaking?" It's really important to recognize whether you're projecting and making assumptions about what's going on right now or will happen in the future, or you're ruminating about what others might be saying. This only causes more stress for you—stress that you might not even realize is affecting your body in many different ways. Work with what you know is true!

Most of all, be kind to yourself. Acknowledge how you're feeling. Then do things that make you feel better. The emotional repercussions can last for some time, and you might not have as much control over them as you'd like quite yet, but you do have control over how you move, how and what you eat, and how you find the time to soothe yourself. This should be a top priority for your health.

WHAT STRESS CAN DO TO YOUR BODY

When the human body is confronted with any kind of stress, it automatically releases two hormones, cortisol and adrenaline, to help you manage it. This release is not something you can control; it's a throwback to our ancestors, who needed to instantly react to danger with a "fight or flight" response to survive. You'll have a physical reaction—a faster pulse and breathing rate, perhaps sweaty palms, agitation, or panic. After the stressful situation resolves itself, the hormones subside and you can breathe normally again.

If the stress continues, however, too much cortisol can be harmful. This is when many of the physical sensations we associate with anxiety arrive—headaches, nervousness, inability to sleep, eating too much or too little, heart palpitations, concentration problems, and more. Over time, these symptoms can even lead to heart disease, diabetes, and metabolic disorders.

How does your body typically respond to a stressful situation?

_____

_____

_____

What do you do to calm yourself?

_____

_____

_____

_____

How long does it take for that to work?

_____

Do you think there's anything else you could do to help manage your stress?

_____

_____

_____

THE STRESS RELIEF YOU NEED

I want to offer a few ideas about free or low-cost stress busters that will not only help you to feel good right now but will improve your overall physical and mental health and well-being into the future. If you have children, you might want to have them participate in some of the non-solitary activities—you'll get the double-whammy benefit of teaching them self-soothing techniques and knowing that you'll have someone to keep you motivated to do fun and empowering activities. Or you might want to ask a friend or two to accompany you, which will also make it less likely for you to cancel. The company of trusted and sympathetic friends can be a huge panacea when you're post-breakup.

You might also want to find some stress busters that are completely different from what you did as a couple. (Of course, if you went running together and you still love to run, don't stop!) That way, you can develop new skills and interests that are wholly your own.

You likely know already about online tutorials. I'm amazed by the depth and breadth of the topics available to stream, and most of them are free. They can teach you how to do just about anything!

What is your favorite stress buster right now?

_____

_____

How often do you use it?

_____

GIVE YOURSELF PERMISSION TO SHOW YOUR FEELINGS

For many people, stress relief means getting it all "out of your system." After a devastating emotional trauma, it's really okay to give yourself permission to do things you normally wouldn't do, such as the following:

- Getting a massage or facial
- Getting the spa mani/pedi
- Eating a gallon of ice cream for dinner (but not more than once!)
- Crying in public
- Yelling at people who cut you off in traffic

What do you give yourself permission to do?

_____

_____

_____

_____

_____

Are you doing something now that you never did in the past? If so, what is it?

_____

_____

_____

What brings you the most comfort?

_____

_____

_____

JOURNALING

Keeping a journal is an incredibly helpful way to get your feelings out—as you're doing with this workbook. It allows you to be as specific and detailed as you want to be about the infidelity and other aspects of your relationship. It's your private place to vent and focus on what you want and need. As time goes by, you'll be able to revisit it if you want to and see how you were feeling at the time, what you chose to write about then (and how important it was), how things have changed, and what you have learned. Any patterns or specific issues will be obvious—and that can be helpful, too.

Don't feel that you have to write in your journal every day. It's there for you when you need it. Some people like to create a gratitude journal, listing the things they are grateful for every day. These can be as simple as waking up in a good mood or getting a call from a friend, or as deeply satisfying as getting a raise at work. Even when you are still feeling the pain of infidelity, there will always be things to be grateful for.

Do you already keep a journal?   *Yes* ☐ *No* ☐

If so, how do you use it?

_____

_____

_____

How helpful is it?

_____

_____

_____

VOLUNTEERING

Not only does volunteering help others, but it can make you appreciative of what you have rather than focusing on what you've lost. You don't need to spend a lot of time or energy (that you may not have) to volunteer. Organizations that need help—especially those for children, seniors, or animals—are grateful for anything you can spare. This is also an excellent way to keep busy and encounter a new set of like-minded individuals and/or activities.

Do you volunteer somewhere already?   Yes ❐ No ❐

If so, how has this helped you?

_____

_____

_____

_____

If not, what would you like to do?

_____

_____

MAKING VISIBLE CHANGES

Why do so many women cut their hair or paint the walls when a relationship ends? Changing your appearance (haircut/makeover/wardrobe redo) can make you feel like a completely different person, because you'll *look* like a new person, as mentioned earlier. The old you had to deal with infidelity and its repercussions. The new you is going out in the world confident about how you look.

Making changes at home can be equally satisfying. Many of my clients have told me they've redone the bedroom and made it into the haven they always wanted. They no longer have to compromise on décor, especially if their ex had insisted on certain items and colors.

What visible changes did you make after your breakup?

_____

_____

_____

_____

Did they make you feel better?   Yes ☐ No ☐

If not, why not?

_____

_____

If you haven't made any visible changes yet, do you plan to do so in the future? What would you like to change?

_____

_____

_____

CREATE PLAYLISTS OF YOUR FAVORITE MUSIC

Music is one of the great mood-changers. It can soothe, invigorate, inspire, and get you moving. Creating playlists of your favorites is a way to make yourself happy. However, you might want to avoid music that reminds you too much of your ex, such as the songs you both loved or songs that were played at your wedding. And don't do what my client Carlotta's neighbor did!

"When I lived in a small apartment building in New York, my upstairs neighbor would come home from work around 6 p.m., throw her bags on the floor, and put on "Every Breath You Take" by The Police on an endless loop," Carlotta told me. "She had gone through a bad breakup, and this was her solace—but it would go on for *hours*. After a few weeks, some of our other neighbors started pounding on her door so it would stop. She didn't care. We felt like having a party when she moved out. Even now I can't hear the singer Sting without cringing!"

If you like to sing, joining a choir is a wonderful way to be surrounded by music, and the group dynamic can be both comforting and exhilarating. Or you could learn how to play an instrument, which is mentally absorbing and empowering as you progress and become more skillful.

Start crafting your stress relief playlist now. What is your go-to music for feeling good?

_____

_____

_____

_____

_____

FINDING THE PHYSICAL EXERCISE YOU LOVE

After an emotional trauma, people sometimes don't want to leave their beds. They have no energy or desire to move—and that is understandable, of course. Yet for everyone, especially those who aren't used to exercising, the actual act of getting your heart rate up will not only be energizing but will be a useful way to soothe jangled nerves and get any negative feelings out of your body.

Human bodies are meant to move; we are animals, after all. According to the Centers for Disease Control and Prevention, "Each week, adults need 150 minutes of moderate-intensity physical activity and two days of muscle strengthening activity, according to the current Physical Activity Guidelines for Americans."[6] Divided by seven, that's not very much, and you don't have to work out all at once. Many people who are pressed for time

---

6 "How much physical activity do adults need?" Centers for Disease Control and Prevention, last modified June 2, 2022, https://www.cdc.gov/physicalactivity/basics/adults/index.html.

just do ten-minute bursts when they can. Strength training can easily be done at home using hand weights.

Physical activity can improve your concentration, memory, and brain health; help you lose or maintain weight; strengthen muscles and bones; strengthen your heart and cardiovascular capacity; reduce the risk of diseases such as diabetes; improve balance; lower blood pressure; help your sleep hygiene; and improve your mood. It's not just a mood-changer, helping to reduce anxiety and depression, but concentrated bursts of aerobic activity (going from a jog to a sprint, for example, or taking a dance class with nonstop moves for several minutes at a time) can tell your brain to release endorphins, the "feel-good" chemicals that flood you with a rush of pleasure. That's something you certainly need right now!

Crucial to any exercise routine is finding something you truly enjoy doing so that you'll stick to it. If you join a local gym, there should be a wide range of exercise machines and equipment as well as classes. There are also countless classes online, especially on YouTube, that you can do in the privacy of your home. If you live in a large city, local meet-up listings will help you find sports/groups in your community, and this is an excellent way to not just get moving but to meet new people.

Doing gentler types of movement, such as tai chi, qigong, and yoga, are good not just for the body but also for the soul, as they involve focused breathing and meditative concentration. And walking, of course, is free. Picking up the pace from a leisurely stroll will give you cardiovascular benefits as well.

While on the topic of movement and health, use this as a reminder to get a full physical. As you've learned already, stress takes a toll on your body. It's especially important to have blood tests done to check on your hormones, which can easily get out of whack, especially if your eating habits have changed or you're not getting enough sleep. Avoid self-diagnosing via Dr. Google or taking a handful of supplements that you might not need in hopes that they'll help. They might, or they might just be a waste of your money and give you unexpected side effects.

What kind of exercise do you do now?

Is this enough to give you the benefits your body needs?   Yes ☐ No ☐

How does exercising make you feel?

_____

_____

_____

If you're not working out now, can you set a specific date to start? When would that be?

_____

Do you have specific goals for your workouts?   Yes ☐ No ☐

If so, list them here.

_____

_____

_____

_____

MEDITATION

There are many kinds of meditation, and you'll know which one is best for you because it'll just *feel* right. Most meditation is merely something you do to clear your mind when the need strikes. You just need a few minutes to find a quiet place and sit or lie down comfortably to meditate and then reap the benefits this mind-soothing and clearing will bring you. Many apps offer music or guided meditations to aid in the process.

Do you have a meditation practice?   Yes ☐ No ☐

If so, how does it help?

_____

_____

_____

If you don't have a meditation practice, is this something that interests you?
Yes ☐ *No* ☐

AFFIRMATIONS, MANTRAS, AND CREATIVE VISUALIZATION

Many people like to write down or memorize affirmations or mantras to say aloud whenever they need a boost of positivity. Sometimes they'll write them on sticky notes and place them where they'll be seen often—the bathroom mirror, the fridge, the nightstand, the car, their handbag, or even a desk drawer at work. These can be useful when you're feeling blue and just want to see something positive. Saying or thinking these thoughts—and believing them—will reinforce the truth behind the words.

Creative visualization is a technique in which you literally envision your plans and hopes for the future. You can create a scenario in your mind or draw it in any medium. This uses the power of your imagination in a positive way and set goals that you hope to reach someday.

Do you have personal affirmations or mantras? *Yes* ☐ *No* ☐

If so, what are they? Write a few here, such as "I will listen to my gut feelings" or "I am strong and capable and worthy of love."

_____

_____

_____

_____

How do they help you?

_____

_____

_____

When are they most useful?

_____

_____

_____

BREATHING TECHNIQUES

When the fight-or-flight instinct kicks in or you're extremely upset about something, controlled breathing really works to slow down your speeding pulse and lessen your agitation. It's simple to do—you just breathe in very slowly for a certain count, then exhale slowly for a certain count. One of the most common patterns is to breathe in for a count of four, then breathe out for a count of seven. It's hard to talk when you're concentrating on breath work, which can also ease a stressful situation. And if you take yoga, focused breathing should be part of what you do in class for soothing relaxation.

Do you have a go-to controlled breathing technique that helps you calm down?
Yes ☐ *No* ☐

If so, how does it help?

_____

_____

_____

CREATING A STRESS-BUSTING PLAN

When you're ready (hopefully today!), draw up a stress-busting plan incorporating activities such as the ones listed above along with any others you have in mind. Just don't beat yourself up if you don't get to them every day. Being proactive with your planning will plant the seeds in your mind so that you'll begin to do these things on a regular basis.

	ACTIVITY 1	ACTIVITY 2	ACTIVITY 3
Daily			
Weekly			
Twice a Week			
Biweekly			
Monthly			
Quarterly			
Every Six Months			
Every Year			

EMPOWERMENT

CHAPTER 9
TURNING LOSS INTO OPPORTUNITY

"No relationship is ever a waste of time. If it didn't bring you what you want, it taught you what you don't want."

—Unknown

One of the most important statements you can tell yourself is this: Just because your relationship ended doesn't mean it was a failure. It didn't have the longevity you wanted, but you couldn't have known that when you and your ex first made a commitment to each other.

Pain distorts everything. When you're in pain, it's hard to feel anything but that awful ache. In the moment, it might have felt (or it still feels) that things would never change. But just as with those euphoric moments we all hope to have in life, the intense pain that comes with infidelity doesn't last, either. You didn't think you could live through this, yet you did. The worst thing that could happen did happen, and you didn't crumble! As time goes by and the pain diminishes, you can get a clearer picture of what happened and your response to it.

If you're at this point in your breakup recover journey, it's a good time to ask yourself these questions:

What do you see differently now than you did initially?

_____

_____

_____

_____

How has the narrative of your relationship changed in your thinking?

_____

_____

_____

_____

_____

Sometimes it takes infidelity for you to realize how unhappy you were. Or *you* might have been happy and thought your ex was happy, too. Some people were content with their lives and their relationships, yet their exes did the one thing that would push things in the wrong direction. The ex could have felt a momentary need for excitement or a change to their routine. They could have felt entitled, for whatever reason. And sometimes they just might not be able to explain why they cheated.

So here you are. Anywhere from weeks to months to a year or more later, able to see the shift in your emotions from the initial shock to now. You've been challenged and hurt, but you've also been able to be honest with yourself. And you've probably developed a profound self-awareness that you might not have had before.

Even if it's taken you quite some time to get to this point, you can now look at the first few chapters of this book and the answers you wrote and be instantly transported back to how you felt when you wrote those answers down. That's why doing all this work is so helpful!

Do any of your initial answers surprise you now? Which ones, specifically?

_____

_____

_____

_____

_____

THE **COURAGE** TO **WALK AWAY**

Why do you find those answers surprising?

_____

_____

_____

_____

_____

How has your perspective shifted over time regarding your experience?

_____

_____

_____

SHIFTING FROM THE PAST
TO PEACE OF MIND

The end of a relationship is life-changing, to be sure, but it isn't *all* bad. Why not? Because it speaks to *your* identity. You now have the chance to define yourself individually rather than as half of a couple.

The first step toward getting somewhere else—past that infidelity marker—is making the conscious decision *not* to remain where you are. Change can be scary initially, but it's not impossible. It's doable. *You* can do it. And it can be life-enhancing in ways you might never have thought possible.

I believe the word *change* has a bad rap. A lot of people hear that word and think about the what-ifs and the negatives, but I want you to flip that so you can see change as emboldening, energizing, and forward-thinking. When we don't resist change—when we step out of our comfort zones—we can surprise ourselves by thriving. Change can become one of the most empowering experiences we'll ever have.

CASE STUDY: AVA STARTS DATING AGAIN

When Ava's ten-year marriage to her college sweetheart ended because of his infidelity, her first thoughts were justifiably panic-stricken. What was she going to do? How would she support herself without her ex's salary? What about their joint accounts and mortgage? Why did he do what he did? Where was she going to live? Would she have someone to be with?

About six months later, after the initial shock wore off and the fear and sadness slowly began to dissipate, Ava told herself she was ready to date again. She went on a lot of dates—simply meeting for coffee—but nothing came of it because she was still thinking about her ex.

"I showed up," she told me, "but I wasn't really *there*. It wasn't fair to the guys I met, either. And then, on yet another date at Starbucks, this perfectly nice guy said to me, 'You know, you seem angry.' He didn't even know I'd just gotten divorced, or really anything about me. So I went home and had a really hard think. I thought I was doing better than I actually was. Some of my friends had told me to jump right back into the dating pool, and it made sense at the time because I wanted to hear that. But some of my other friends had kind of been gently urging me to take a bit more time. They told me I needed that time instead of having a rebound for the sake of a rebound."

Gradually Ava stopped looking at herself as a failure but as someone *in transition*—no longer identifying herself as a person who'd been left, but as a person with opportunities that hadn't existed before. Her mindset about her capabilities and expectations completely changed. When she eventually started dating nine months after that "angry" coffee date, her goal wasn't to have a serious relationship. Her goal was to have fun and enjoy meeting new people. Giving off that vibe of contentment attracted exactly the kind of life-enhancing people she wanted to be with.

LIMITATIONS IN YOUR PREVIOUS RELATIONSHIP

What didn't you do—or felt you couldn't do—while you were in your previous relationship? Every relationship involves balance, with one person usually having to give something up at some point to serve the needs of their partner, and vice versa. This

THE **COURAGE** TO **WALK AWAY**

could be something fairly innocuous, like putting off an evening art class because your ex had to work late on a big project for a month and you couldn't find a babysitter, or it could be something much bigger, like having to stop your studies for an advanced degree when your partner lost their job due to drug abuse.

Perhaps your partner didn't like your friends and made it clear that you couldn't invite them over. Or made comments about your workouts, or your family. It can be incredibly healing to recognize any rigidity and limitations you'd accepted in your previous relationship.

List the things you gave up because your ex wanted you to do so.

_____

_____

_____

_____

_____

_____

Was that an ask or a demand from your ex? How was it phrased?

_____

_____

_____

Was your ex willing to give up something that really bothered you? If so, what?

_____

_____

_____

Did your ex make you feel bad for asking?   Yes ☐ No ☐

What were you willing to settle for, if anything?

_____

_____

_____

_____

WHAT'S DIFFERENT NOW ABOUT YOUR WANTS AND NEEDS?

When you were with your ex, you might have had a rigid checklist (written in indelible ink) of things you thought you absolutely had to have in order to be half of a happy couple. Married by thirty, a nice house by thirty-one, baby number one by thirty-two, new shoes every three months, a beach vacation every nine months… and the list goes on.

I've seen many people who were utterly crushed when their checklist items with their ex remained unchecked. Part of the *bad*, as it were, of ending a once-loving relationship is losing what you once needed. The *good* can be recognizing that those wants are no longer needs. And they're no longer so important.

It's time for you to think about what you really want and what you really need. Instead of making a checklist, which can be limiting and steer you in the wrong direction, try framing certain things as deal-breakers instead. Take all your newly found experience, self-evaluation, and wisdom, and identify what are truly the most important things you want in a relationship (not the small stuff), and what would be unacceptable to you in the future.

We all have different things that we value, want, and need. Yours are unique to you, and you should never feel that you have to defend your choices. What might be extremely important to you might not make sense to others. Everyone has their own emotional history, desires, and budget for being able to go after what they want. It's all relative. Just be aware that you *don't* want to turn these deal-breakers into a litany of must-haves or must-dos solely because you didn't have them in your previous relationship.

In what ways, since your relationship ended, are you better aware of who you are and what you want?

_____

_____

_____

_____

What do you think are your responsibilities regarding your own happiness?

_____

_____

_____

What was important to you in terms of your morals and values when you were still with your ex?

_____

_____

_____

_____

What did you think you needed the very most at that time?

_____

_____

_____

_____

If you did get what you needed most (a house or children, for example), was it satisfying in the ways you'd hoped or expected?   Yes ☐ No ☐

Or was it surprisingly disappointing? If so, why?

_____

_____

_____

_____

What was the hardest thing to lose because you broke up?

_____

_____

_____

_____

_____

Are you now better at discerning which things are necessities, which are wants, and which are luxuries?   Yes ☐ No ☐

HOW TO STOP LOOKING BACKWARD

It can be awfully hard to let go—not just of a relationship, but of many aspects of life. We all have things we wish we'd done, and some of us are still kicking ourselves mentally with what-ifs and why-didn't-I, years or even decades later. I don't think it's an unfair generalization to say that practically everybody has a natural tendency to make comparisons, and this makes sense when buying a toaster oven or a new car. But comparisons shouldn't be made with people, as this can trigger the what-ifs. As much as you might want to compare your ex with the dates you go on post-breakup, it is important that you don't compare people in the present with the person in your past. You have changed since you picked your ex, and someone you date now is much more likely to be a reflection of how you've changed.

There's no timeline for looking forward rather than dwelling on the past; this can take months or even years. Yes, of course you want to look back to learn from any mistakes or denials, but that isn't the same as looking back to romanticize the good while downplaying the bad. It's okay to admit how much you miss certain aspects of life with your ex. Maybe you traveled a lot, or relished the intimacy of your sex life, or enjoyed sparring with each other in spirited conversation. Or maybe you just loved being part of a couple. Or you were thrilled that within the confines of marriage, there was a security blanket of not having to wonder what you'd be doing at night, and with whom.

Romanticizing can help take the pain out of your memories, but you don't want to dwell only on the beginning of your relationship with your ex (when things were blissful) or on its end (when things were not). Either viewpoint is an extreme; life really takes place in the middle. You also might not have realized how little space there was for you with your ex, not understanding how dim the lights were in that relationship until you were forced by infidelity and its aftermath to get a new, brighter bulb. That diminishment might have been so slow and insidious that you only recognized it once it was truly out of your life.

No person can move forward while still looking back at what had been. The perseveration trap of the *why-why-why* can be a deep one. You can unconsciously be putting your life on hold and stunting the possibilities of a better future.

The truth is that you may never know the *why*, and your ex might never know, either! If you keep waiting and waiting for an answer, trying to find out the details because not knowing is driving you crazy, the answers you get will likely never be satisfying. Infidelity always starts off as a secret, and very often it ends with a secret—just a different kind. When you get to the point when you realize you don't want to know and don't need to know the *why*—and, more important, *it doesn't matter anymore*—well, when you can let go of that, you are moving forward in a very positive way.

This shift in perspective takes place once the pain and anger are reduced or put in perspective. Once you've worked through those feelings, then you can see what's possible for your future. Instead of the emotional suffocation that looking backward brings, you can take the noose off and breathe freely!

When you look back on your past relationship, what feelings arise?

_____

_____

_____

_____

Do you think you might be over-romanticizing certain aspects of life with your ex?
Yes ☐ No ☐

If so, what are they?

_____

_____

_____

_____

If there were long-standing issues with your ex, can you now see how much tension or frustration you were living with?

_____

_____

_____

_____

Are you relieved that your ex is now your ex? Yes ☐ No ☐

If yes, how does that relief make you feel?

_____

_____

_____

_____

Looking back, what are a few elements in your past relationship that you want in a new relationship?

_____

_____

_____

_____

REDISCOVERING WHO YOU ARE

While being half of a couple has some wonderful aspects, so does being on your own. This is especially true if you had a relationship in which there was a lot of compromising on your part. All relationships involve some level of compromise, but sometimes—without your even realizing it—the compromising can become so insidious and you can get so worn down that you give in just to get along. But if you are no longer putting your ex's needs before your own, you will have far more emotional energy for yourself.

Instead of asking yourself "What do I want to do today?" ask "What *can* I do today?" While asking that question, also ask yourself what you'd like to accomplish that will make you feel good when you look back on it.

Did any compromises you made with your ex bother you a little, a lot, or intensely?

COMPROMISES MADE	BOTHERED A LITTLE	BOTHERED A LOT	BOTHERED INTENSELY
	❑	❑	❑
	❑	❑	❑
	❑	❑	❑
	❑	❑	❑
	❑	❑	❑

COMPROMISES MADE	BOTHERED A LITTLE	BOTHERED A LOT	BOTHERED INTENSELY
	☐	☐	☐
	☐	☐	☐

If you did make some difficult compromises, how do you feel now that you're done with them?

_____

_____

_____

_____

STOP ROMANTICIZING THE PAST WITH YOUR EX

Instead of romanticizing the past, here are a few things that you might do instead.

- Make decisions the way *you* want to make them.

- Get a lease or a mortgage in your name only.

- Set up a new bank account with custom checks that have the starfish image you always liked.

- Buy the car you always wanted, in your favorite color.

- Eat what you like instead of cooking what your ex wanted (no more overcooked pasta).

- Remember that you no longer have constant fights leaving you drained and unhappy.

- Go out with friends after work instead of going home and making dinner.
- Travel someplace your ex never wanted to go to.
- Remember, you no longer need to pretend around super-critical in-laws or family members.
- Enjoy sleeping deeply without being woken up.
- Hang out with your friend's new puppy (which you couldn't do before because your ex was allergic).
- Have fun with hobbies you had put off before.

Do something you haven't done before! The end of one stage of your life is the beginning of another one. Your focus now should be on opening up your world.

What do you now have time to do that you didn't before? List as many things as you can think of.

_____

_____

_____

_____

_____

_____

_____

_____

_____

What do you want to do first, and why?

_____

_____

_____

What activities or hobbies have you always wanted to do but weren't able to do before?

_____

_____

_____

_____

_____

Have you been able to do some of them recently?   Yes ☐ No ☐

If so, how has doing these activities made you feel?

_____

_____

_____

If not, will be you able to find the time soon?

_____

_____

YOUR FUTURE RELATIONSHIPS

The gradual diminishment of your post-infidelity pain has no set timeline, and there's no set timeline for being ready to have another relationship, either. Everyone will want and need some time on their own to adjust, to deal with the emotional fallout as well as the logistics of uncoupling. Be kind to yourself. Do what you need to do for *you*.

WHEN ARE YOU READY TO DATE?

After a committed relationship ends, some people are truly happy never living with someone or getting married again, and they are content having future relationships strictly on their own terms. Others hope to find another intimate partner fairly quickly. Still others might be so busy with work commitments or children that they understandably want to concentrate on those aspects of life for the present. What's important is to not pressure yourself about wanting to meet someone new.

Your friends are likely sharing their opinions about whether or not you should start dating, but only you will know when you're really ready—and you may not know until you actually do it. I've had clients who didn't want to go on any dates five years after their divorce was final. I've had others who set up an online dating profile and were actively looking to date three weeks after the discovery of infidelity. Some jumped back in when they weren't ready just to validate their attractiveness, or simply because it was difficult for them to be on their own. People who moved in together or married when young might not have much experience with living on their own. It can be frightening and overwhelming for those who don't know how to be alone.

Most people will think about dating again, perhaps talk about it a bit with friends and family, and then just go for it. Start with something that has an easy cutoff, like a coffee date. After eight ounces of coffee, you'll know whether this is someone you want to see again! And, of course, you might go on a few dates and then, like Ava (page 144), realize you're not *there* yet. If so, be proud of your self-awareness, push back your dating plans for a while, and have fun doing whatever else pleases you most.

If after some time you're feeling stuck, however, the tough question you'll want to ask yourself is this: Am I resistant to another relationship because I'm afraid? Is the thought of dating terrifying? You'll want to challenge this. Usually fear is about the unknown. It is helpful to challenge the fear you feel. Are your fears real, or are they being framed as the worst thing that could happen? Uncovering what you're afraid of can open the path to moving forward.

Is having another long-term relationship or marriage one of your goals? Why or why not?

_____

_____

_____

How do you know that you're ready to date again?

_____

_____

_____

_____

_____

Are you looking for fun, or for a more intense relationship?

_____

_____

Or are you just looking for something to do to stave off loneliness?

_____

_____

If you're not ready to date, why not? (It will help to clarify your reasons.)

_____

_____

_____

_____

Are you fearful of something specific?

_____

_____

_____

Are you just not ready to deal with someone emotionally? Yes ☐ No ☐

Are you so busy taking care of your new circumstances that you don't yet have the energy or the inclination to date? Yes ☐ No ☐

If so, do you think these circumstances might change anytime soon? Yes ☐ No ☐

I AM READY TO DATE BECAUSE...

Here are some suggestions for knowing when you're ready to date:

- You can honestly say that the reason you're dating is *not* that you're scared to be alone.

- When you hear about your ex, you tune out because you really don't care.

- You are way past needing to talk about your ex, especially when you're on a date!

- You know how much you have to offer someone new.

- You feel excited about sharing aspects of your life with someone else. You're not scared of it or dreading it.

- You feel excited and hopeful about the future.

WHAT *NOT* TO DO ON A DATE

One of the biggest turnoffs on a date is to start talking...and talking...about your ex. It means that you're spending this date thinking about your ex instead of the person you're with. If you have children, of course you should mention them—but don't take out your phone and show forty photos of last week's school play. That's probably not the tone you want to set on a date.

If your date asks questions about your ex, shy away from the details—at least until you get to know the person better. You are fully capable of coming up with just a brief summary. Remember that when you are talking about your ex, you are also talking about yourself. What do you want your date to know, or exactly what do you feel comfortable talking about on a first date?

You certainly don't want to listen to your date complaining about a previous relationship or saying, "I wasted my life with that person, because they...." If they only talk about themselves, that is probably how they generally interact. Tell them something about yourself, and hopefully they will ask you a question in return. If they don't, be glad you are only meeting for coffee! If a first date isn't good, some people are willing to give them a second chance, in case they were nervous or having a bad day. But what you see is often what you get.

WHAT ABOUT A FUTURE PARTNER?

When thinking about a future partner, it can help to be brutally honest and identify the qualities your ex had (positive/negative, endearing/drove you bonkers) and why you were attracted to them. If your ex was living life on the edge and full of fantastic plans that somehow never came to pass, that may initially have been extremely attractive—but the thrill wore off when you found yourself carrying all the responsibilities in the relationship. Obviously you're far more aware of that personality type now than when you were in the heady, early days of your relationship. If you've lived with someone who turned out to be difficult, you've doubtless become hyperaware of the signs of immaturity, selfishness, and a controlling personality.

This perspective will allow you to define the emotional, intellectual, spiritual, and physical qualities you're looking for in future relationships. Let this knowledge inform your decisions about potential mates, but don't let it *dictate* your decisions. I think it's fair to say that we all want a partner who complements who we are, someone who's trustworthy, loving, kind, and generous—who just *gets* us. An ideal meeting of hearts and minds. But that kind of relationship is something that develops over time.

After all, first impressions can be misleading, or they can be wholly indicative of what a person is like. When first meeting someone, it's common to fill in the blanks of their personality, especially if the date has gone well. Filling in the blanks is more about what *you* want in the person and less about who *they* are. For example, the person you meet might not be very talkative, so you think they're not interesting. Yet it turns out they're just very shy, but actually smart and passionate about certain topics. Or the person you meet might be an extrovert who is sexy and great in bed while conveniently forgetting to tell you about the person whose bed they shared the night before. You never can tell what someone is truly all about unless you spend considerable time getting to know them.

The point I'm trying to make is to never say never. One of my clients was married to a cop who became unfaithful. "I'm never ever getting involved with another cop," she told me, shaking her head vigorously. "It was so stressful worrying and wondering about his safety every time he went to work." Well, you guessed it. She fell in love with another cop, and she decided he was worth the worry!

What attracted you to your ex?

_____

_____

_____

_____

List their good qualities.

_____

_____

_____

_____

_____

_____

List the not-so-good qualities you were willing to overlook.

_____

_____

_____

_____

_____

_____

What were your relationship blind spots?

_____

_____

_____

_____

Were there qualities you thought were important but now realize weren't? What were they?

_____

_____

_____

_____

What qualities do you want again in a partner?

_____

_____

_____

_____

What qualities are you willing to overlook? (For example, he may not earn as much money in his field as you do in yours, but he is valued, compassionate, and a hard worker.)

_____

_____

_____

_____

What behaviors might be automatic deal-breakers—such as drinking, taking drugs, being cagey about their relationship with their children, offering to pay but always forgetting their wallet, being rude to the help... and so on?

_____

_____

_____

_____

_____

CAN YOU REMAIN FRIENDS WITH YOUR EX?

As time goes by, some people think they're going to be able to stay friends with their ex, while others have no desire to speak to them ever again. It is not a requirement to be friends with your ex. The first time you met you weren't yet friends, were you?

If you can't handle hearing about whom your ex is dating, then you can't be friends. That can change, of course. Ex-couples sometimes can become friends over time, when healing has taken place and they are no longer invested emotionally in each other in the same way. For example, you might be extremely happy in a new relationship with someone you trust, or happy to be on your own, and past hurts have mellowed into memories that no longer have the power to sting. Your ex might be somebody you want to keep in your orbit, though obviously in a different way. After the healing process begins, you may discover that your ex is a far better friend than partner and may have changed in unexpected positive ways. And if you have children, you'll always want to do your utmost to be amicable, to minimize stress for everyone.

MOVING FORWARD WITH HOPE

"I thought that the biggest failure would be my marriage ending," Megan said to me. "But the infidelity had already happened, and there were the things my husband had done, the things that were his fault. But *mine* is a success story, because despite mistakes along the way, I got out. I protected myself. And my children."

Even if your relationship ended badly, it was still an important part of your life. That it ended doesn't make it any less important or make you a failure. In other words, infidelity wasn't the whole relationship. That doesn't define the marriage—or you, for that matter. Yes, there was infidelity, but there were so many other aspects of your relationship that shaped who you are today in the best of ways.

The goal is not just to meet somebody better or completely different than your ex. The goal is to fulfill yourself. That could mean finding a new romantic partner or some amazing new friends. Or it could mean going back to school for an advanced degree— something you always wanted to do, but your ex's job always came first. It could mean that you move across the country, or change careers entirely. It could mean that you decide to be a single parent. The opportunities awaiting you are endless!

See yourself as a work in progress. Take your emotional temperature. Check in with yourself.

Here's what I'd like you to be in the process of doing:

- Moving forward to acceptance of what happened
- Taking responsibility for whatever you need to take responsibility for
- Being curious about what is now possible
- Transitioning into life without your ex
- Recognizing that fear is common during major life changes—and that you can deal with it
- Opening yourself up to new friends and situations
- Trusting yourself and others (just because your ex wasn't trustworthy, that doesn't mean that others aren't!)
- Reframing negative thoughts and looking back at what was good in your relationship so you can identify the positives and seek them out again, if you so desire
- Refocusing on yourself

Do you see yourself in this list?   *Yes* ❏ *No* ❏

Is there something missing from the list that you'd like to add? Write it down here.

_____

_____

_____

Is there something on the list that is still hard for you? If so, why do you think that is so?

_____

_____

_____

Remember, if you were in a relationship with your ex for ten years, you are now ten years older than when the two of you started your life together. You have lived through the ups and downs of an intimate relationship. You are not the same person now as you were then. You are older, more experienced, and certainly wiser.

GOALS FOR THE FUTURE

Start setting your future goals now. When you write these goals in the space below, try to think that you are writing them as *intentions*. (Relationship goals can be like having a checklist of very specific things, and that can get in the way of what you're really looking for—you don't want to check yourself out of having any future partnerships!) Let's say you're going shopping to buy a red shirt. In every store you enter, you focus only on red shirts because that's what you want—so you don't even see the other shirts. Setting intentions works in your subconscious, guiding you toward your goals but allowing you to see other possibilities along the way.

Goals for next week

_____   _____

_____   _____

_____   _____

Goals for next month

_____   _____

_____   _____

_____   _____

_____   _____

Goals for the next quarter

_____   _____

_____   _____

_____   _____

_____   _____

Goals for the next six months

_____   _____

_____   _____

_____   _____

_____   _____

Goals for the coming year

_____   _____

_____   _____

_____   _____

_____   _____

THE **COURAGE** TO **WALK AWAY**

IN CONCLUSION

I've asked you a lot of questions in this book—and you've answered them, as painful or as empowering as that might have been! Keep reminding yourself of your intentions and wishes and where you want to go in your life. Life gets busy, and we can forget about ourselves and our needs, getting caught up in the demands of daily responsibilities. Step back and give yourself the kudos you deserve for the time and energy and honesty that you've put into this book.

Is there still a question that comes to mind that wasn't asked? If so, what is it?

_____

_____

_____

What hasn't been covered for you?

_____

_____

_____

Where and how do you want to continue moving forward past your breakup? (Think of that as your further reading section when you finish this workbook!)

_____

_____

_____

Always remember: The courage to walk away is also the courage to answer questions the only way you know how—by being you!

ACKNOWLEDGMENTS

I am especially grateful to my literary agent, Todd Shuster, at Aevitas Creative Management. Special thanks to Jack Haug and Lauren Liebow at Aevitas. Many thanks to the entire team at Ulysses Press, especially Kierra Sondereker, my editor, who asked me to write this and guided me in the process. Thank you to Phyllis Elving, who copyedited the manuscript.

Thanks to my grandparents, Pauline and Max Bell, who planted the seeds of love and nurturing that I needed. And thanks to my mother, who thought I could do anything if I worked hard enough.

Thanks to the brilliant Karen Moline, who brought my thoughts and experiences to life.

I am eternally grateful to Judy Levitz, PhD, founding director of the Psychoanalytic Psychotherapy Study Center in New York, who enriched my professional life as a mentor and supervisor.

My thanks for the endless empathy and generosity of spirit of Roberta Ross, who suggested I write a book when it was only a dream. To Caryn Breen, for her perspective when I needed it most. To Luisa Riano Anderson, who inspires me with her wit and ability to say it how it is. To my sister Robin, who has supported me throughout my life. I am also grateful to Dalia for her encouragement, her ability to see the big picture, and her guidance throughout. To my son Jordan, who inspires me to follow my heart as he does his. To my son Brett, whose strength and independence rivals only his love for his family. And to my daughter-in-law Christa, who made space for me in her family as she joined and enhances mine.

ABOUT THE AUTHOR

© Deborah Feingold

Lisa Brateman, LCSW, is a psychotherapist, relationship specialist, public speaker, and media commentator with more than two decades of experience. She offers individual, couples, and group therapy in New York City. Her areas of expertise include anxiety and depression, couples therapy—marital and premarital—and conflict resolution. She earned her bachelor's degree in communications from William Paterson University and her master's degree in social work from New York University.

Lisa is a contributing member of SheSource at the Women's Media Center, a progressive, nonpartisan, nonprofit organization working to raise the visibility, viability, and decision-making power of women and girls in media. As an internationally recognized expert in her field, Lisa is a frequent commentator for TV, radio, newspapers, and magazines. Analyzing the psychological impact of current events, Lisa demystifies human behavior and relationships.

In addition to her private practice, Lisa served as psychotherapy consultant at the office of New York Sinus and Sleep Medicine, where she worked with clients to reduce anxiety and other psychological barriers to sleep. She has offered therapy groups on women's issues at the NYC Community Center. She has been an adjunct professor in social work and sociology at Saint Thomas Aquinas College in Sparkill, New York, teaching a course entitled "Social Work in Today's World."

Her second book, *What Are You Really Fighting About? How to Turn Conflicts into Conversations*, will be published by Rowman & Littlefield in 2024.

The mother of two sons, she lives with her partner in Manhattan.